Mike —
y

God's Promises

Every One Fulfilled
He Is Faithful
You Can Count on It!

www.godspromisesfulfilled.com

Glen Aubrey

Creative
Team
Publishing

Creative Team Publishing
Fort Worth, Texas

Disclaimers:

Due diligence has been exercised to obtain written permission for use of references, quotes, or imagery where required. Any additional quotes, references, or imagery may be subject to the Fair Use Doctrine. Where additional references, quotes, or imagery may require source credit, upon written certification that such a claim is accurate, credit for use will be noted on this website: **www.godspromisesfulfilled.com**

- o The opinions and conclusions expressed herein are solely those of the author and/or the individuals and entities represented. This book is unashamedly a book of religious faith in God, and reliance upon Him as Sovereign Lord, trusting His promises.
- o Views and opinions are quoted with permission, and are presented without regard to any political affiliation(s). Opinions and conclusions of Contributors are limited to their telling of the facts, experiences, and circumstances involved.
- o No professional, psychological, or medical advice is implied, stated, or offered in any way whatsoever. You are encouraged to seek professional help, education, advice,

and counsel from individuals you deem competent should you desire to learn more about the topics covered.

o Note: certain names and related circumstances may have been changed to protect confidentiality. All stories where names are mentioned are used with the permission of the parties involved, if applicable. Any resemblance to past or current people, places, circumstances, or events is purely coincidental.

Scripture:

o All Scripture references are quoted from the New International Version (NIV) of the Holy Bible, unless otherwise noted. **New International Version (NIV) Copyright © 1973, 1978, 1984, 2011 by Biblica**

Website Design: Randy Beck www.mydomaintools.com
Cover design: Justin Aubrey

Special thanks are given to Frank and Gerri Pownall for their inspiration for the imagery of the front cover.

ISBN: 978-1-7350189-9-7

PUBLISHED BY CREATIVE TEAM PUBLISHING
www.CreativeTeamPublishing.com
Ft. Worth, Texas
Printed in the United States of America

God's Promises

Every One Fulfilled
He Is Faithful
You Can Count on It!

Glen Aubrey

Contents

Contents

Contents

*****

Endorsement and Foreword

Dr. Jim Garlow
CEO – Well Versed
www.WellVersedWorld.org

Glen Aubrey and I have had prized association and networking since the early 2000s. We have been friends personally, and associates in ministry professionally throughout the intervening years.

I contributed a farming illustration for Glen's inclusion when he wrote his book *Core Teams Work * Their Principles and Practices* in 2007. Now Glen has written a new work: *God's Promises * Every One Fulfilled*, for the believers and followers of Jesus Christ, showing how God's faithfulness is evidenced in everyday life.

I enthusiastically endorse Glen Aubrey. I know him. You will want to read anything he writes. His goal is to encourage your growing dependence on the Lord of Life, and His plans for you.

~ Dr. Jim Garlow, CEO – Well Versed, 2021

Opening Introduction

Monica Hunter
Family Friend

I have had the privilege of knowing Glen Aubrey for twenty years through my mentoring friendship with his exceptional daughter, Heather. When Glen told me he was working on a book about God's promises, I was pleased but not surprised, since I know Glen to be a Kingdom-minded man.

In fact, one of the most prominent ways I have seen God's promises play out in his life is in the lives of his children and grandchildren. Glen raised his children in the "disciplined instruction that comes from the Lord" (Ephesians 6:4), faithfully sowing God's love and truth into their souls from the time they were tiny. Proverbs 22:6 promises this: "Train up a child in the way he should go: and when he is old, he will not depart from it." (KJV)
~ King James Authorized Version, Public Domain

I know Heather well, and for a long time now. I know Glen's son, Justin, by reputation, and I know both Heather and Justin's spouses as they have been long time family friends. Heather and Justin have both faithfully walked with the Lord and both are committed, devout Christian believers with a super abundance of fruit in their lives.

They both married equal and like-minded, beautiful, passionate partners, and are raising thriving passionate God-fearing and God-loving children.

When I think of God's goodness and promises in the life of Glen, I think also of his work in the context of this verse, Ephesians 2:10: "For we are God's handiwork, created in Christ Jesus to do good works which God prepared in advance for us to do." (NIV)

Glen is unusually gifted by the Lord in multiple areas, some of which are music, language, administration, interpersonal communication, and teaching. Glen has always used his gifts to bless and help people; to bring them joy, to inspire them, to help them be better in all manner of ways, and to assist them in expressing themselves and getting their helpful messages out. He has been particularly passionate about messages that align us with the culture of heaven and move us into the light of God's love and truth.

All of that is to say: there are striking ways God's promises are beautifully displayed, and His sovereignty and presence are revealed in the life and legacy of Glen Aubrey.

~ Monica Hunter, November, 2021

Prelude

Psalm 138:8
A Psalm of David

8 The LORD will work out his plans for my life—for your faithful love, O LORD, endures forever. (NLT)

The undeniable truth of the scripture above is summed up in this phrase: "endures forever." How much of anything really endures *forever* and how can that assertion be proven?

Consider content and intent of all human interactions and conversations, the totality of men's and women's activities; and in business: banks, stores, distribution centers; in nature: plants and animals, mountains, valleys, rivers, oceans, even earth itself; and in our Universe: planets, solar systems, asteroids; and in our world: national governments; any and all buildings including homes, marble edifices, huge cathedrals, sky scrapers including the Twin Towers in New York (World Trade Center) …

What can be declared to last for *all* time and eternity?

The answer, of course, is this: while some things do indeed last a very long time, can we surely declare that any will last forever? From a human perspective, of course, we will never know "forever" while we are here on earth; we won't be around long enough to experience complete fulfillment in all things.

Consider promises: how about promises made to you, from you, to others, from others? How will we know for certain that promises made by anyone will become promises kept and fulfilled? How do the results of promises endure? In fulfillment, can any be truly counted on, infallibly?

We humans are not eternal in life on earth, obviously … we are subject to forces beyond our control including our futures and eventual death; yet, we hear, receive, and make promises constantly. Can every human promise made be one that is fulfilled?

Promises, promises, promises … we are inundated with them, and we hear them all the time, either by association, or personally. Promises are parts of the fabric that compose all aspects of families, networks, and business.

Politicians spit out promises whenever they want our vote. In dealings with medical professionals, hired vendors from gardeners to painters, participants in weddings, "commitments" to donations and pledges, promises are uttered and often not fulfilled, sometimes intentionally, other times, not.

Promises require trust from the giver and receiver if they are to be deemed reliable. In what or whom do you place your confidence? According to Wikipedia: "On July 30, 1956, the 84th Congress passed a joint resolution 'declaring **IN GOD WE TRUST** the national motto of the United States.'" Thank God for this resolution: the government at least got that one right.

> Promises require trust from the giver and receiver if they are to be deemed reliable.

Recently a close friend and mentor asked, "Who can you trust?" It's a good question. And it has an answer.

Simply put, you and I can, and must, trust God. He has never failed to honor His commitments. He is faithful, and we can count on it!

Our opening scripture began with, "The LORD will work out his plans for my life ..." Note the word, "will." This speaks to an ongoing process, not a conclusion already experienced, though the conclusion is sure when God is working on our behalf.

Prelude

The bottom line: <u>God's faithful love endures forever,</u> <u>through *every* process which involves us.</u> We can rely on that truth. That fact alone is cause enough to put our lives in God's hands. David declared, "God is working out His plans for my life." To what degree do you have that personal assurance?

Confront the obvious: not everyone accepts this assurance personally; some, in fact, are diametrically opposed to God's words. Even when up against testimony from those who do not believe, no matter how large and loud these groups may be, what God says is unshakable.

From Romans, 3:3-4 (AMPC), even if …

> [3] "… some did not believe and were without faith … Does their lack of faith and their faithlessness nullify and make ineffective and void the faithfulness of God and His fidelity to His Word?" The writer of Romans goes on to answer his own question: [4] "By no means! Let God be found true though every human being is false and a liar …" God's word remains true, even in front of "sinful men …" a judging audience of unbelievers.
> Amplified Bible, Classic Edition (AMPC)
> Copyright © 1954, 1958, 1962, 1964, 1965, 1987 by The Lockman Foundation

Conclusion: What God says *is* dependable, period. That means it can be counted on by anyone, anywhere; including promises made and promises kept.

In God Alone

The history of Divine dealings with human beings is replete with promises *made* and promises *kept*. In the composition of the Bible itself, we read promises declared and ultimately, faithfully fulfilled, sometimes centuries apart. The proofs are undeniable in scripture. In my Bible for study every morning from the New International Version (NIV), footnotes throughout scripture point up fulfillment, listing the exact scripture where a promise was first declared. It's remarkable. Not one promise was left undone.

One of the clearest examples of God's Promises was made to Abraham (over a hundred years old) regarding his wife, Sarah, who, though past child-bearing years, was promised: she will give birth to a son. See Romans 4:20 and 21. Abraham's faith was noted here: look at his great faith in the Promises of God (emphasis by author):

> [20] Yet he did not waver through unbelief regarding the promise of God, but was strengthened in his faith and gave glory to God, [21] being *fully persuaded* that God had power to do what he had promised.

God came through: Isaac was born. This was one example of hundreds.

*****

God's fulfilled promises and His eternal love are undeniable in contemporary human history, too. Many of these modern examples are recorded in the accounts in this book. My account is one of them.

True stories related here are living and lasting testimonies to the indelible fact of the follow-through of God Almighty in the lives of real people, proven in space and time. God's reliability is not a theory, a wish, or an imagined dream. It's real ... which is why it is deemed "reliable."

I invite you to read accounts of God's presence: Matthew 28:20b: "I am with you always ..." and presents: gifts, grace, and blessings. James 4:6: "... he gives us more grace." The evidence of God's presence and presents is shared in the lives of our book's Contributors, all of whom I have had the unique and special privilege of knowing personally and, in many cases, professionally.

So, what literally "endures forever?" Specifically, David, the author of the opening Psalm, says it is "...your faithful love, O LORD, endures forever." What lasts: God's faithful love. "Forever" has no limits, and "endurance" is ultimate strength.

Do God's promises affect us and surpass all time? We are told that God is love (1 John 4:8), and we know He sent Jesus to die and redeem us. He did this because He loved us (1 John 3:16-18) and commanded us to love one another (1 John 4:9-12). Ask: can we depend on the lasting truth of God's love? I say we can. Will you join me in that belief?

Note that David, the Psalmist, used the phrase, "faithful love" which means it endures. According to Romans, nothing can separate us from God's love that is in Christ Jesus our Lord. (Romans 8:38 and 39) This means you and I can count on God's love, always, and in all ways.

Read on …

*****

Selected Scriptures: God's Promises

Joshua 21:45

Not one of all the LORD's good promises to Israel failed; every one was fulfilled.

Joshua 23:14

"Now I am about to go the way of all the earth. You know with all your heart and soul that not one of all the good promises the LORD your God gave you has failed. Every promise has been fulfilled; not one has failed."

1 Kings 8:56

"Praise be to the LORD, who has given rest to his people Israel just as he promised. Not one word has failed of all the good promises he gave through his servant Moses."

Psalm 119:140

Your promises have been thoroughly tested, and your servant loves them.

Psalm 145:13

Your kingdom is an everlasting kingdom, and your dominion endures through all generations. The LORD is trustworthy in all he promises and faithful in all he does.

Romans 15:8

For I tell you that Christ has become a servant of the Jews on behalf of God's truth, so that the promises made to the patriarchs might be confirmed

2 Corinthians 1:20

For no matter how many promises God has made, they are "Yes" in Christ. And so through him the "Amen" is spoken by us to the glory of God.

2 Peter 1:4

Through these he has given us his very great and precious promises, so that through them you may participate in the divine nature, having escaped the corruption in the world caused by evil desires.

> Can you and I completely and unreservedly trust the promises of God? Absolutely, "Yes!"
> **Every promise has been fulfilled.**

2 Peter 3:9 [Emphasis by the author]

The Lord is not slow in keeping his promise, as some understand slowness. <u>Instead he is patient with you, not wanting anyone to perish, but everyone to come to repentance</u>.

The Bible is a book of redemption. The Promises of God are proclaimed with one purpose: to redeem human beings. Belief in that truth requires faith. Redemption is possible through God's grace alone.

Ephesians 2:8 and 9:

> [8] For it is by grace you have been saved, through faith—and this is not from yourselves, it is the gift of God—[9] not by works, so that no one can boast.

*****

There is an old gospel song, the lyrics of which go like this (various renditions exist, all are Public Domain):

> "Ev'ry promise in the book is mine,
> Ev'ry chapter, ev'ry verse, ev'ry line.
> I am trusting in His love Divine,
> Ev'ry promise in the book is mine."

Starting when I was quite young, my mother and father used to sing this at church, coupled with other gospel poems/songs. Clearly, these lines stuck with me. The words express a fundamental and lasting truth on which we can depend.

As you read each true account on the following pages, you will instantaneously recognize a definitive trend: God is gracious, faithful, and honors His commitments, each and every one, all the time. These stories are all about fulfillment of God's promises for our good.

The movie collection from **National Geographic** starring Morgan Freeman, entitled, **The Story of God** (Seasons One and Two) seeks to examine faith system origins and beliefs from many religions, world-wide. It is a well-produced account of varied beliefs and practices, including stories of near-death experiences. The collection endeavors to present perspectives unique to each faith system, including but not limited to faith and practices of Christians, Jews, Arabs, members of the native American tribe often called Navaho Indians, Hindus, Buddhists, the Mayan culture, and other ancient religions as well.

While educational, and I encourage its acquisition for general knowledge, one thing is lacking (in my opinion). It is this: the God of the Bible is a personal God who declared clear and unmistakable promises, and fulfilled them ... each and every one. No promise was not fulfilled. No other faith system can say that and prove it.

Set Apart ... Holy

Perhaps the greatest promise and fulfillment upon which the Christian faith rests, is Jesus Christ: His birth, life, teachings, crucifixion, and resurrection. That fulfilled story sets Biblical faith apart. It demands our attention and ultimately, our devotion.

*****

God's Promises in One Life

Glen Aubrey
Author, Publisher

Early in my college days (1970 – 1974), I deliberately chose a verse in Psalms as a "life verse." "Life verse" was the term we used to describe any verse that was selected to set the tone and perspective for all activities, and I applied it personally for who I was. Back then I did not know how meaningful this verse would be in my life. The word, "meaningful" doesn't do it justice even now. I still claim this passage today as a central verse for my soul. It has literally framed important life choices.

The verse is Psalm 118:14. In the King James Version (KJV) which was the version of the Bible on which I was raised, this scripture says,

> 14 The LORD is my strength and song, and is become my salvation.
> ~ Public Domain

Let me unpack this for you in simple terms. The sequential order of the terms to describe the LORD is important. First, however, the term "LORD" meant that I gave and still give my full allegiance to His rule and reign in my life. There would be no other I would ever serve.

The verse begins with "strength" as a characteristic of the LORD. I was then, and still am, a highly driven individual, one who plans meticulously, a goal-setter, a high achiever and, at times, one who pushed *hard* (maybe too hard, as I have learned, but more on that in a minute).

It felt like there was nothing I could not accomplish for God in my personal endeavors, both religious and secular, when I believed I was functioning within the will of God, striving to obey Him.

Recounting the multitudes of instances where I relied on God and myself, empowered through Him, would not serve us well here; but all of this drive really began in elementary school. I was told by my parents if I received straight A's in the sixth grade, that upon completion of that achievement, my parents would purchase me a Conn Organ, Artist Version, with an American Guild of Organist (AGO) pedalboard. This reward was to compliment successes already achieved in the field of music, particularly piano performance, original song writing, and leadership of vocal groups.

Well, it happened.

My father purchased this classic organ, and for years we had both the original piano (Story & Clark) and that organ virtually side by side in our home in La Mesa, California. Looking back, I must have learned that if I tried hard enough apparently success would follow.

On the Creative Team Publishing website (www.creativeteampublishing.com), I present blogs. The one for August, 2021, is telling. Let me illustrate "drive" by recounting here this blog that features two incidents not in any way related to music; rather, speech (forensics: original oratory and oratorical analysis), and victories in speech tournaments during high school years.

I hasten to add: I was *not* perfect in any way. But successes in these competitive speech tournaments continued; in two marked cases, interspersed with family tragedy.

The blog for August, 2021, edited, is initially addressed to authors who are writing for Creative Team Publishing, or considering doing so:

Three Times the Prep for One Presentation
© 2021 by Glen Aubrey. All Rights Reserved.

I learned a *long* time ago that there were no substitutes for preparation for any presentation in which I was to be engaged. This habit of being prepared started in high school, in speech tournament preparations and music rehearsals. Preparation is essential. So is research. ***Thorough*** research. And yes, thorough preparation takes time and requires effort.

This need for in-depth preparation continues today, perhaps more now than ever before. How many times in the news media are we given conflicting reports, some of which are downright incorrect or positioned to sway opinion and not deliver truth? Just recently an author of ours questioned: who and what can you believe?

If you are a writer who is considering publishing your work, we can all agree that preparation is essential, because it is. In the case of a writer, preparation activities often include research as well as being committed to these principles:

1. Truth. Your desire to communicate must be anchored in Truth.
2. People sources, personal and written: who are they and why do you reference them?
3. Desire to get details correct: "Just the facts, ma'am; just the facts ..." The facts have to be accurate in context, dates, and contents.
4. Embellish only if you tell your readers you are doing this ... exercise honesty.
5. If you quote *anyone* or reference *any* quote, be sure to not steal or plagiarize; obtain written permission from a person or publisher.

6. Set a higher standard for accuracy.
7. Following scripture, "speak the truth in love." (Ephesians 4:15, KJV)
8. Concern yourself with the details, because generally no one will be as concerned about your work, at least at first, as you are and must be.
9. Part of research is presenting your findings with correct grammar, punctuation, and spelling. Be a stickler for doing it right.

The list doesn't stop there. You get the idea.

A true story: in my first speech tournament in high school, as a freshman, I learned a life lesson that stuck. It's a permanent, rock-solid truth. Here's the backstory: I possessed some natural God-given talent for which, sincerely, I was grateful. I had been complimented in Junior High, and began my freshman year (Grossmont High School, La Mesa, California) with high hopes to do well in forensics. I was referred to, and became part of Grossmont's Speech Team. In my very first speech tournament at Palomar City College in San Diego County, I was able to win two first place trophies, one in Original Oratory (OO) and one in Oratorical Analysis (OA). That kind of victory appeared unique, and I basked in the moment. That is until I came in on the Monday following the Saturday tournament and walked up to my speech coach's desk with the two first place trophies: one in each hand. His one and only

comment at first set me back: "You're not that good."
Silence. Yes, on the surface it hit me hard. On
reflection, however, the coach was 100% right. Coach
Plum, who was a master communicator himself, had
nailed it even though I didn't realize it at the time.
I resolved to work hard, and did. In fact, I prepared
and strove diligently to become better from that time
forward. Thank you, Dick Plum, for this life-changing
life lesson!

What did this resolution mean for a high school
student? Hard, time-consuming labor, taking the God-
given talents I had and earnestly trying to perfect these
through four years of high school. The efforts worked.
In my sophomore year, 1968, when I was 16, I won the
Optimist International Oratorical Contest out of 40,000
entries nationally, all boys. The finals were held in
Louisville, Kentucky.

An important point: in my first year of entering the
Optimist International Oratorical Contest, 1967, at age
15, I made it to the semi-finals (Portland, Oregon), and
bombed. A red phone was used to allow me to call and
inform my sponsoring club (La Mesa Optimist), that
I still had one more year of age eligibility, and I told
them I would try again. That choice, of course, meant
starting completely over. So, I did.

This tournament had iron-clad requirements:

1. A speech could be no more than five minutes.
2. It had to be memorized.
3. A contestant had to win first at each level to remain as a competitor.

Then in 1970, my senior year, I entered the Lion's International Speech Tournament and took first place nationally out of about the same number of entries, girls and boys. Same requirements as above.

An important part of this story has to be inserted here. In my junior year (1969), my older sister, Joan, who did not live in our home, committed suicide; it was a drug-induced addiction that finally took her life. She had "blown her mind" on speed (the vernacular of the time). This composed a rollercoaster set of circumstances for the family, to say the least; in fact, that expression doesn't begin to describe the full range of emotions we endured, especially those of my dad. It was the first time I had seen him cry. For me: from an ecstasy in winning nationally, with news coverage, trips, and accolades, to a tragedy in my sister's untimely death, Joan's passing was sandwiched in between markedly pivotal years of high school. Yet, sorrow, as deep as it was, and even still is today in memory, would not be allowed to derail personal and appropriate ambition.

The point? There is no need for any applause here; wisdom will say, instead, that greater desires for good and fulfilling a God-given work ethic, while accepting the finality of losing a family member, should build character and resolve in the long run. We don't ever deny sadness; we won't let it consume us, however; that's the intent.

In all the speech tournament success, preparation could never be assumed. Ever. If a goal was to be set, I concluded, I *must* prepare, and then prepare some more.

How much preparation is needed to be the best? I have generally found that the amount of prep effort required is at **least** three times the effort in performing any actual presentation, be it in person, or in print, including performances in music.

Be encouraged in your pursuits. Mine is just one story. No victory comes minus sacrifice. Every victory absolutely requires hard work, no matter what. Note: these efforts are **not** just for the presenter, either; rather, they are really *for those who will receive your presentation*. How much do and must we care about our audiences?

Question: how willing are you and I to work hard for something for which we believe God has gifted us? If we possess an opportunity to achieve, especially an achievement for His glory and honor, let's give it our all.

Just for the record regarding speech tournament successes: the Optimist speech title was: "The Golden Opportunities of Youth." The Lion's speech title was: "Generation Gap: Fact or Fantasy?" The titles seemed appropriate for the time.

Your titles and contents of books and presentations carry important weights and responsibilities today. Strive well to prepare and present.

You are worth it. So is your audience.

*****

Talk about drive! I was deeply motivated, achieving successes while enduring immense tragedy, and this drive continued all through my first jobs preceding and upon college graduation. These job positions accented and provided outlets for communication, and especially for my music which by that time had become a personal driving force and an exceptional tool.

Remember, we began by considering "strength." According to our "life verse," the second characteristic of the LORD is "song." This was so true in ministry and secular recording endeavors beginning in 1976, continuing for decades. With fifty + songs published, nationally produced record albums (preceding cassettes and CD's), and presentations to literally thousands of people in a vast array of audiences, eventually I chose and designed programming arts consulting, doing this for ten years. "Programming Arts" may be a new term for you. It simply meant forming teams of people who present music, media, drama, technical services, support services, stage design, and administration. My job literally was to "work myself out of job" by training a PAD (Programming Arts Director) who would lead these teams for every organization with which I consulted. Participants in the organizations which retained me (mainly churches large and small, and conference camps) numbered in the thousands. The successes were remarkable.

These achievements gave birth to original book writing and publishing, beginning with *Leadership Is — How to Build Your Legacy, Industrial Strength Solutions * Build Successful Work Teams*, and *Core Teams Work Their Principles and Practices*. These books led to others of mine and books from other authors ... more than 80 books in print.

These first three books of mine were used extensively in what became fulltime business, government, and non-profit consulting, literally all over the United States. Client list included West Point (United States Military Academy), Whirlpool, California State, San Diego County and city government (Fresno, California), local and national media outlets, and more.

Plus, a family! My wife, Cindy, and I were proud to raise one daughter, Heather, and one son, Justin. One vital aspect through all the involvement in consulting, music, and publishing was *dating* my children, a monthly endeavor fully supported by Cindy. Beginning when Heather was six years old and Justin, at age four, I dated each child monthly until they left our home to be married. I treasured these times! Now, Heather's husband carries on these date events with their five boys, and Justin does as well with his three girls.

The dates are described in **Industrial Strength Solutions * Build Successful Work Teams,** beginning on page 235. So, I was hugely busy and loved it all, trying to achieve a healthy balance between work and family. Add winning an Emmy ® in 2012 for a commercial for a company based in San Diego known as Postal Annex +. This commercial can be accessed on www.glenaubrey.com, courtesy of the executive producer [Thank you, Steve!]. Along with thousands of hours of studio recording, music writing, and production (thousands of songs, thousands of pages of original music manuscripts), there were few spare moments of inactivity.

After a move to Texas from California, all that "driven-ness" came crashing down in 2019. I learned that for years (some estimates are up to twenty of more) I had been suffering from hypertension, high blood pressure (apparently an inheritance from my dad, who passed in 1982) to excessive limits, and simply had not known it. We'll forgo all the details for now; suffice to say that to my knowledge and memory, I had never endured such a physical crash as I did in 2019. Then COVID-19 occurred (again, this is an estimation but a reasonable diagnosis by family that I had contracted it) right at the beginning of 2020, before we knew much about the virus. An extremely *s-l-o-w* recovery was experienced over eight weeks. With help from families from a local church, support and prayers from family, recovery began and strength gradually returned. Recuperation continues through the grace of God. Plus, diet, exercise, and lifestyle changes have brought renewed strength and vitality.

Part of the physical damage inflicted with hypertension was seen in kidney dysfunction, predating 2019. At the outset (2017 – 2018), the lab numbers were not good at all. Personal progress ensued to right this wrong, coupled with much prayer and complete lifestyle alterations. Lab results received in early 2021 revealed that the kidneys *were actually being restored.* Was I shocked and profoundly grateful to God, friends, and family? Yes. I had been told that kidneys could not be rejuvenated. But the lab numbers didn't lie. They showed marked and continuing improvement. Another of our authors, a registered nurse, said she had never seen such positive numbers (2021)! Attending a follow-up appointment with my nephrologist (kidney doctor), he asked (basically my words, relating his question), "To what do you attribute these numbers and the obvious improvement?" To which I replied,

"Well, I take a tremendous number of vitamins, and I am a man of faith, trusting God." He offered no reply, except, "Keep doing what you are doing." Basically, identical sentiments were echoed by my primary care doctor. Further, another of our authors who had received a kidney transplant several years ago, who is a firm believer in God and the efficacy of healing in God's power, said he was amazed. Well, we all were.

God is active! He heals, He restores. I am living proof of that!

I gratefully extend credit to Dr. Rick Redd, MD, a strong believer in God, and a practitioner of traditional as well as holistic medicine, who is also one of our most recent Creative Team Publishing authors, for his perspectives and advice. He is a new friend, and his council which I requested and have followed wholeheartedly, has literally turned my condition around.

I *strongly* encourage and invite you to acquire his book and study guide at this website: www.all-inornothing.com. The title of his main book is ***All-In Or Nothing * Master Your Destiny***.

Plus, one additional chronic (my word, my description) challenge occurred without warning in May of 2021: I experienced vision issues which greatly concerned me. Without reservation, I called and asked for prayer from believing authors, family, and friends. They prayed! After two visits to an ophthalmologist and an understanding local prescription provider, those issues were resolved. Talk about thankful, *again*, I am!

> God is active! He heals, He restores.
> I am living proof of that!

I would be remiss without mentioning my next-door neighbors (last name withheld). I have never known more giving people than Josh and his wife. Their care and true friendship continue to astound me. I am a recipient of their care and help consistently. Undoubtedly, moving in close to them was God-ordained.

These are all examples of the third characteristic of the LORD expressed in Psalm 118:14, which is "salvation." God's salvation comes through Divine intervention and often through His people. I have personally witnessed and experienced both.

Literally, the verse says that He *"has become"* my salvation. How true, how true.

I am told that at the outset of the hypertension episode, I easily could have died, had a heart attack, or a stroke. These conditions did not occur, I am convinced, because of the grace and gifting of God.

Deliberate adjustments in lifestyle, including diet, exercise (bike riding, many times up to five miles daily), and more, were not easy. They're still not easy, but determination (drive) has kicked in again!

Couple this with natural aging, there is one word I will share here which sums up the situation for me, a word which I have used countless times in the last three years. That word is **_grateful_** … to God, family, friends, and acquaintances. So, so grateful!

In summary: the verse quoted again from Psalm 118:14 …

> 14 The LORD is my **strength** and **song**, and is become my **salvation**.

*****

Many years ago (during early college years), I wrote an original worship song entitled **Reflect**. The music style reflected the trend of the times.

Lyrics:

Pause a moment and reflect
On what the Lord has done for you,
With a heart that's filled with praise,
In the Spirit of love and truth.

(1)   Think of the blessings that you've received
And the fullness of His presence since you've believed;
Think of His gifts of love and grace:
These are things we can't replace.

(2)   Life is the greatest within His will,
And the future He has promised is better still!
Jesus gave all so you and I
Now may live and never die.

Pause a moment and reflect
On what the Lord has done for you,
With a heart that's filled with praise,
In the Spirit of love and truth.

A scan of the original music follows:

Personal reflections are birthed from God's sustaining grace, His love, truth, and more. I continue to rely on Him and His power. Victories belong to Him; not me. I give God *all* the glory and honor.

The conclusion of this chapter: in willful reliance and total dependance upon God, I trust His will for my life, His upholding **strength, song,** and **salvation**. These were His promises to me, borrowed from the Psalms. Truly a "life verse." God has never failed. He will never fail you, either. We can count on it!

> Victories belong to Him; not me.
> I give God *all* the glory and honor.

*****

Contributors and Their Stories

Mike Atkinson, Publisher: *Mikey's Funnies*
Title: *When Good Is Not Good*

Judy Bowen, Author: *Riding the Fence Really Hurts!*
Title: *He's a Good, Good Father*

Janine Cushman, Internal Marketing Consultant,
     National Food Company, Minnesota, United States
Title: *Make Someone's Day*

Jack Elwood, Executive Director, Heal Africa, USA
Title: *Carol's Story * Divine Faithfulness*
     Amidst Human Suffering

Richard (Rick) Fleming, Author: *Living Faith ***
     Inspiring Stories to Encourage You
Title: *God — A Part of Everyday Life*

Robert Glenn, Author: *Rearing Up America ***
     The Journal of a Father's Reflection on Special Needs
Title: *God's Sustaining Grace*

Vernon Lintvedt,
Pastor, Blessed Savior Lutheran Church, O'Fallon, Illinois
Marty Lintvedt,
Licensed Professional Counselor
Title: *God's Power Is Promised To Pull Us Through Every Difficult Climb, and Overcome Every Stubborn Obstacle*

Rick Redd, MD, Author: *All-In Or Nothing * Master Your Destiny* and *All-In Or Nothing * Beyond Retirement*
Title: *My Child, Did You Know?*

Nancy Sidock, Poetess
Title: *God Has No Down Time*

Skip Vaccarello, Author: *Finding God in Silicon Valley * Spiritual Journeys In A High Tech World*
Title: *God Never Gave Up on Me*

Larry Wolf, Retired L.A. County Sheriff, Criminal Justice Professor, University of Antelope Valley, Lancaster, California
Author: *A Black and White Decision, Policing Peace,* and *Word on the Street*
Title: *Challenges of God's Faithfulness*

When Good Is Not Good

Mike Atkinson
Publisher: *Mikey's Funnies*

We had just finished praying for our loved ones who were leaving to move across country. As they pulled away, one of the trailer tires blew. Of course, frustration was our first reaction. And our second reaction came as we realized they didn't get the correct tools to change a tire on a heavy trailer.

A quick run around town to get the tire fixed and to get the correct tools, and they were back on their way in an hour.

As my wife, Stacy, and I reflected, we remembered praying for God's safety and protection on them as they traveled. The irony is that the request was answered within moments. You see, if they had left with no problems, that tire (which had a nail in it) could have blown in the middle of the desert, a long way from the services and stores he would need to get it fixed.

So, the good we prayed would befall them was actually answered with an immediate popped tire. In our limited view at the time, we didn't see that as good, but as an untimely inconvenience.

This memory brings me to my favorite promise of God from James 1:17, New Living Translation, NLT:

> "Whatever is good and perfect is a gift coming
> down to us from God our Father, who created
> all the lights in the heavens. He never changes
> or casts a shifting shadow."

~ *Holy Bible*, New Living Translation, copyright © 1996, 2004, 2015 by Tyndale House Foundation. Used by permission of Tyndale House Publishers, Inc., Carol Stream, Illinois 60188. All rights reserved.

My understanding of this verse has evolved through my life. But it wasn't until I experienced a life-threatening disease that I realized the pivotal word in this promise is "good."

I reflected on that word and realized that my perspective of it had always been from my limited, earthly view of "good," – not God's definition.

So, what is His definition?

No Coincidence

Of course, we know that a single Bible verse can rarely stand alone. The Holy Spirit, through the chosen writers, communicated connected truths before and after a verse.

James did not bury the lead in his opening of this letter to Jewish believers, James 1:2-3, NLT:

"Dear brothers and sisters, when troubles of any
kind come your way, consider it an opportunity
for great joy. For you know that when your faith
is tested, your endurance has a chance to grow."

Not exactly an upbeat opening message. But it was
obviously what those early believers needed to hear, and
certainly we do, as well.

Here are five main points James makes as he wrote the
verse we're considering:

1. Welcome tribulation.
2. Ask God for wisdom.
3. The importance of humility
4. God blesses patience.
5. God does not tempt us.

I've always been drawn to the book of James because it
focuses on action, behaviors, and maturity. These first few
verses are filled with the kind of direction we need, to get
through each day.

Our reaction to hard times should be to focus on God and
His goodness. He gives us wisdom, teaches us to exercise
humility, and blesses our patience and endurance.

And then this from James 1:16, NLT:

"So don't be misled, my dear brothers and sisters."

This admonition precedes his proclamation that every good and perfect thing comes directly from the Father.

Divine Parking Spots?

So, does that mean God really did give me that good parking spot?

"The hand of God didn't wrap that coffee mug your friend so kindly gave you, nor did He hold the crayon that so sweetly drew the rainbow now hanging on your fridge, but He is, in an ultimate sense, the source of all that is good. So, when we receive a gift from a loved one, we can not only appreciate the love coming from them; we can also look beyond it to feel divine love flowing through them."
~ Jessica Udall, Crosswalk
https://www.crosswalk.com/faith/bible-study/how-does-every-good-and-perfect-gift-come-from-above.html

This is the definition of "good" that we expect: good job, good family, good house, etc. And, yes, these *are* good gifts and thus worthy of a spirit of thankfulness toward our Heavenly Father.

But in a heavenly perspective, good can also mean the result of testing and tribulations we encounter – loss of job, house, family, etc. Those things happen to good Christians around the world every day.

"James regarded trials as inevitable. He said *when,* not *if* you fall into various trials. At the same time, trials and tests are occasions for joy, not discouraged resignation. We can count it all joy in the midst of trials because they are used to produce patience … **Of course, the ultimate goodness of any gift must be measured on an eternal scale.**"
(Enduring Word commentary; emphasis mine)
https://enduringword.com/bible-commentary/james-1/

As I look back on the last few years of suffering, pain, and upheaval due to my disease, I have come to the conclusion that I am truly thankful for it all. While I wince at the dark times, I know that God has worked His ways into my developing maturity.

In time this knowledge brought humble gratefulness for His mercy and correction.

According to His Purpose

This realization leads right into a more well-known verse, written by the Apostle Paul, Romans 8:28, NLT:

"And we know that God causes everything to work together for the good of those who love God and are called according to his purpose for them."

Everything: the pleasant to the hard. I didn't fully realize this until He carried me through the last few years of troubles.

God didn't promise us a life without problems. He promised to draw near through them, to give us wisdom as we choose humility, and to bless our patience.

May we learn

To see His definition of

"good" gifts in our lives.

From Mike:

While Glen and I had known each other from our days at Youth for Christ, it wasn't until many years later that we reconnected in a deeper way. I had been laid off from a fourteen-year job, so I decided to start my own business, which I had never done before.

In the time since Youth for Christ, Glen had become a business consultant in great demand. He patiently mentored me through the next couple of years of struggling through this new career path, which helped me immensely.

But more importantly, Glen has become a dear friend. Our spirits share many experiences and we support each other through the bumps and windy paths of life – praying for, and encouraging each other.

~ Mike Atkinson, January, 2022

From Glen:

Mike Atkinson and I met in the 70s at San Diego Youth for Christ. He and his wife, Stacy, have been dear friends for many years. I so appreciate his contributions in my life!

More recently, every week day I enjoy receiving his email publications he has titled, *Mikey's Funnies*, in existence now for twenty-six years! While this Christian humor and clean publication is received in many countries throughout the world, each *Funny* and corresponding *Thot* not only present clean humor; they also often carry inspirational themes as well. Subscribe to receive the publication (it's *free*) at www.mikeysfunnies.com.

Through it all, literally "all," Mike's faith is unwavering, his honesty inspiring, his trust in our Lord's ultimate design for all of us, unmatched.

I consider Mike to be one of my closest and most treasured confidants.

~ Glen Aubrey, January, 2022

*****

He's a Good, Good Father

Judy Bowen
Author: *Riding the Fence Really Hurts!*
Published by Creative Team Publishing
www.creativeteampublishing.com © 2021
Available through www.judy-bowen.com

I asked the women in the Bible Study group that I teach what they remembered most about their fathers and how their fathers impacted their lives. There were many sweet stories about dads that taught them how to play sports and showed up at every game. Or the dad that drove a truck for a living and worked hard, but was always cheerful and never let on that the family was struggling to make ends meet. Fun dads that laughed and played and the dad that neighborhood kids wanted to be around. Dads that loved God and taught Sunday school (that was my dad) and was a good listener. Dads that could fix anything or build cool stuff.

Some dads had passed away and tears were shed in telling of their passing and how much they were missed and cherished. When I asked the question, not knowing if all the gals grew up with a dad, I also added, "If you didn't have an earthly father, tell us about how your Heavenly Father has impacted your life."

Only one of the women in the group didn't grow up with a dad in her life and was raised in a cult with her mom and siblings. This gal always has a smile on her face, and was gentle, kind, and sweet. She talked about God's faithfulness in keeping her safe and revealing to her the real truth about who He is and how much He loves her. She left the cult, along with her soon-to-be husband, and they both serve the Lord and attend our church.

More and more stories poured out relating the faithfulness of our earthly dads and how blessed we felt to have them in our lives. This made it easy to talk about the faithfulness of our Heavenly Father. Among God's provisions:

1. His watchful eye was ever over us.
2. He kept us from harm and comforted us.
3. He provided us with jobs, money to pay bills, and buy food.
4. He healed us from health issues, divorces, and addictions.
5. He opened the door for us to return to Him when we strayed.
6. He provided caring friends.
7. He acquainted us with a Bible teaching church.

On and on we can say without a doubt, "He's a good, good Father!"

> He will cover you with His feathers, and under His wings
> you will find refuge;
> His faithfulness will be your shield and rampart.
> Psalm 91:4

*****

I'm not sure what I was expecting the first time I checked in with the guard after walking through a metal detector and handing over my driver's license in exchange for an entry badge. As I was led down the long cold hallways, I could see cracks in the cement floors that were old and patched up many times. The walls were dirty and empty of any pictures or signs of life. The strong smell of cleaning products permeated the stagnant air. Then came the long hall of tiny cells with locked doors, a bed, sink, and toilet inside. Sometimes a pair of plastic slip-on sandals were left outside the locked door. There were guards everywhere in uniform.

I finally made it to Unit 700, a girls' unit, where I was led into a large barren classroom of sorts. There was a guard station inside and three or four female guards. The desks were set far apart. The young girls lined up to come in from their cells, each with their hands tucked securely under their arms at all times. All were dressed in the same issued uniform: dark blue knee length shorts, dark blue T-shirts, dark knee-high socks, and brown plastic slip-on sandals. Each girl sat by herself around the room in assigned seating. The intimidating guard firmly reminded them that this was "church" and they were to be respectful. If they demonstrated disrespect, they would be taken back to their cell. I wanted to hug each one of them but that was not allowed.

It has been my joy and an answer to prayer to be invited into Juvenile Hall to teach a Bible Study to these young girls every other week. They were incarcerated, scared, ashamed, with very low self-esteem, desperately in need of love, forgiveness, hope, desperately in need of JESUS! I prayed, "Come, Holy Spirit, and do Your thing ... speak through me into their hurting hearts, help them to understand that You love them, You're their Heavenly Father, and You have an abundant life for them if they will surrender to You and accept Your love and forgiveness. Everyone else may have failed them but You won't. Please let them know they can trust You!"

We had one hour and I asked them to read from the paraphrased "Teen Bible" we teach from. It's alarming how poorly they read, stumbling over simple words; and they know almost nothing about Jesus or the stories in the Bible. They asked sweet questions (always raising their hand to be called on as instructed) and listened closely as I explained characters and stories, reminding them that God used flawed and disobedient people all through the Bible to get His message out, and He still does! I reminded them that God is a life changer, and regardless of what they've done, He loves them deeply.

Of course, there are always girls that reluctantly come to "church" and are full of anger. They have no intention of participating. This was the case recently as I watched this particular young girl arguing with the guard about being falsely accused of something she said she didn't do. She was told to sit down in the back, and the issue would be dealt with later. She buried her head down in her arms on her desk and wouldn't look up.

I went over to her and told her I knew she was upset and I was so sorry, but perhaps God knew she needed to be there and that she would feel better after we reviewed the book of Psalms and David's life. Surprisingly, towards the end, she raised her hand and said she wanted a turn to read. She was a good reader and also had some answers to questions I was asking. I knew the Holy Spirit was at work!

As always, I asked the girls to bow their heads at the end, and asked them if they wanted to receive Jesus into their heart to pray the sinner's prayer, to themselves (not out loud), in the privacy of their hearts. As heads were still bowed, I asked them to raise their hand if they prayed the prayer. Each time they all raise their hand. I continued to pray "Lord Jesus, please let them know how much I love them, how very much You love them and want the best for them. Amen."

When heads were raised, I could see tears streaming down the face of the girl who came in so angry and didn't want to be there. She said, "That is the first time in a really long time that someone said they loved me. She turned and walked back to her cell. Tears were now welling up in my eyes as I thanked God again for being a good, good Father!

Jesus said, "Let the little children come to me and do not hinder them, for the kingdom of heaven belongs to such as these." Matthew 19:14

Although I accepted Jesus as my sweet Lord and Savior when I was nine years old, and grew up in a Christian, loving family, I wasn't always an obedient daughter to Him. Marrying at eighteen right out of high school to a controlling man was an action I knew I shouldn't have done. I had an affair to get out of the marriage. I remarried a year later to someone struggling with addiction; that marriage lasted nine years.

I engaged in relationships in between that were ungodly as I tested the world for fun and adventure. Raising two children on my own, barely making ends meet for five years, I finally fell to my knees in surrender and returned into the loving arms of Jesus. That is when God blessed me with my wonderful husband (31 years now), and my new "obedient" life in Christ really blossomed. Even in my disobedience I would continue to pray and talk to God, asking for forgiveness and help. He was *always* there, providing me with unexpected checks in the mail, an opportunity to start a new career and make more money, and the support of a loving family who was always there to help. For example, my mom would surprise me with a fridge full of food, or new shoes and clothes for the kids when she could see we were in need. God continued to bless us through her!

He continues to show His faithfulness as I've been through two bouts with cancer over the past eight years and have been cancer free (without chemo, just radiation, a personal choice) for almost five years.

> My health may fail and my spirit may grow weak, but God remains the strength of my heart; he is mine forever. Psalm 73:26 (NLT)

~*Holy Bible*, New Living Translation, copyright © 1996, 2004, 2015 by Tyndale House Foundation. Used by permission of Tyndale House Publishers, Inc., Carol Stream, Illinois 60188. All rights reserved.

There have been other struggles and valleys, but these are nothing God can't get us through if we trust and do not fear, keeping our eyes focused on Him, remembering His faithfulness in the past and knowing He and only He knows our future. He promises an *abundant* life, but I've learned that I must let Him lead, not be influenced and led by the world, friends, family, or media.

Proverbs 3: 5 and 6: [5] Trust in the LORD with all your heart, And lean not on your own understanding; [6] In all your ways acknowledge Him, And He shall direct your paths. (NKJV)

As I look back on my 70 years of life, I know I could fill books with *all* the times God has been faithful to me, protected me, chastised me, tested me, delivered me, directed me, forgave me, and loved me unconditionally. His arms were always open wide to welcome me back when I strayed, never leaving me or forsaking me.

I recently wrote a book, my autobiography, entitled **Riding the Fence Really Hurts**. It goes into detail about my journey of jumping on and off the fence, sometimes into the world, sometimes committed to God. The book chronicles the many times I tried to keep one foot in the world and the other following God's plan. My prayer is that many will relate to my story and be led back to fully being committed to staying in God's plan, His wonderful, exciting, and abundant plan.

As I remembered *so* many fun, heartwarming, frustrating, and hard times, I also remembered my Heavenly Father's faithfulness and love for me, never varying at all, continually wanting to welcome me back into His arms. He's waiting for you to return to the fold, too! He's a Good, Good Father! His promises never fail!

> Judy's book, ***Riding the Fence Really Hurts,*** is published by
> Creative Team Publishing,
> www.creativeteampublishing.com
> and is available through www.judy-bowen.com.

*****

From Judy:

I had the privilege of meeting Glen Aubrey in late 2001 when I was made General Manager of the Salem radio stations in San Diego. He worked with our staff in creating mission and vision statements, good communication skills between departments, making sure the right personnel were in the right positions, and helping me navigate all the new responsibilities I had to deal with as GM.

We hit it off right away and his upbeat attitude and fun outlook on life made it easy to follow his lead. It also was cool knowing we both played the piano and were lovers of music. He even blessed us with a piano concert one evening in our home for family and friends.

I consider Glen a "forever friend" and someone that always has my best interest at heart. Now that's a keeper! Thanks Glen, for all your guidance, patience, and faith in me!

~ Judy Bowen, July, 2021

From Glen:

Judy Bowen has been an inspiration to me, upholding truth, leading her staff, seeking the best ways to accomplish her mission. Throughout changes in her career, she sought God faithfully, as she no longer rode a fence of indecision. God was ever a part of her involvement with people. When times and circumstances presented challenges, she worked for best solutions for all concerned. The term "forever friend" resonates. Indeed, she is that.

~ Glen Aubrey, July, 2021

*****

Make Someone's Day

Janine Cushman

Internal Marketing Consultant,
National Food Company, Minnesota, United States

> The Lord loves us and provides for us, every time …
> all the time …
> without fail.

He blesses us with what we need, but He often has to work through us humans, to deliver. I have often said, "Friends are God's way of taking care of us." It is true for all of us. God uses us to take care of each other.

> God uses us to take care of each other.

What is our purpose? We often ask ourselves this question. We can think it may be something really big like:

1. Cure a disease.
2. Provide peace to the world.
3. Save the turtles.

The list of complicated life dedicating purposes goes on and on.

I believe my purpose and that of many others is, simply, making someone's day. It's my goal and purpose each and every day. 'Seems way less daunting when it becomes something I can do every day.

Even on the days that aren't going so well, or I'm exhausted, I can at least cross this one thing off my list, which starts like this most days ...

1. Brush teeth.
2. Drink coffee.
3. Make bed.
4. Make Someone's Day.

The list goes on and on, each day ...

God knows what you and I need, and I believe He uses me to deliver that to others. This may sound a little conceited, or definitely not humble. But I don't think I'm Jonah, Moses, David, or any other Biblical person. Just like I tell my small group kiddos on Sunday mornings, "God uses us in different ways. He can use all of us and we can make a difference in someone's life." This is a part of God's fulfilling His promises to us all.

> This is a part of God's fulfilling His promises to us all.

It's an amazing tradeoff. I give the Lord all the credit and I get all the joy.

How does this happen? Well, making someone's day usually makes my day.

A recent post from the Mayo Clinic stated that kindness has been shown to increase self-esteem, empathy, compassion, and improve your mood. It's good for the body and the mind. Physiologically, kindness can positively change your brain. Being kind boosts serotonin and dopamine, which are neurotransmitters in the brain. These give us feelings of satisfaction and well-being. They also release endorphins, which are our body's natural pain killer. ~https://www.mayoclinichealthsystem.org/hometown-health/speaking-of-health/the-art-of-kindness

Some would call these "random acts of kindness," but it's not random to me and it's not random to the Lord. Showing kindness is intentional, honest, and grounded in true love. Just as the Lord asked us to do so often in the Bible, specifically in Matthew 22:39b: "Love your neighbor as yourself." Now, more than ever, we need to spread love and kindness, Jesus' love and kindness.

Loving your neighbor can seem difficult, but here are a few examples of ways you can make your neighbor's day that don't require too much effort on your part, but can make a world of difference. Imagine that: doing something good for someone else, and doing something good for your mind and body, too!

Here's my list:

1. **Smile**.

Yes, that's it. Sometimes just a smile is all you need. It fills you up and lets out the light; and in most cases makes the other person smile. Smiling is contagious. Try it. Smile, even when you may not want to; it will help you get through the moments of your days. Smile when you are in traffic or a parking lot, waiting for a spot. Believe it or not, smiling will ease tension and the other drivers will see your kindness through the smile. Who knows: you may even get that parking spot!

Just the other day, my daughter was running a 5K. It was a hot and humid Texas morning and she was miserable; but she smiled most of the race. The race was an "out and back" race so you are passing other race participants as you pound the pavement. After the race was over, an older gentleman came up to my daughter and said, "Seeing your smile and bright eyes kept me moving forward. Thanks for sharing your smile with me." Try it. Smile at someone you don't know.

Now, take it a little further. Bless all with your directed smile. If you let someone in the car lane, smile and bless their drive home. When you hold a door open for someone, smile and bless their day.

2. Pray.

When giving blood, pray during the session. Pray that the blood provides health and strength to those who receive it.

When delivering food or packing food boxes, pray that the food provides the nourishment that is needed.

I find I am constantly praying. It helps me be focused and kind with intent. It draws me closer to the Lord. We are in constant conversation.

I had to think about it at first: stop, pray, and bless, but now I think it's a habit. I don't even think about it much anymore.

My kids will ask me, "Mom, what are you doing?" "Hello? Mom??" If I pause in the grocery store or while driving, I pray because sometimes you can tell a person for whom you say a prayer just needs a little more prayer than someone else.

3. **Be present and listen**.

There is a professional athlete, author, health and fitness expert, DWTS (Dancing with the Stars) champion, who is a celebrity for sure. Every time I have an interaction with him, he always makes my day, not because of his status or accomplishments; rather, because he makes me and everyone else he encounters, feel like they are the only persons in the room when talking or listening to them.

We may be in a fieldhouse filled with kids and parents: it's busy, with loud voices, whistles, people walking all around. But every time he talks to someone, he uses eye contact, a smile, and seems sincerely interested. In conversations like these, I'm sure he may have heard the story before or may disagree with the comment, but that man makes you feel like you matter. I always walk away from the conversation or interaction standing taller, smiling bigger, and feeling better, just because he gave me his presence, he gave me his attention.

I started challenging myself to do the same. I knew how I felt walking away from our interactions and wanted to give that feeling to others. It's hard sometimes, but I try to really listen, make eye contact and, if appropriate, touch the person I am talking to. You can really make someone's day by just giving them your time and undivided attention.

4. **Say their name**.

This one was really hard for me. But I noticed that when someone remembered *my* name, it meant a lot to me. I have a tough name to remember. "Janine" can be hard to recall because it's not a very common name.

But when someone remembered my name, it made me feel good. I try hard remembering the names of the people I meet. I'm not always successful, but I do try. If I forget, I ask again. Then I repeat it to help me remember.

I often try to get the name of our server or the person on the other end of the line helping me make appointments or such. I try to ask them by name when I would like a drink refill or thank them by name for their help over the phone.

It's not much, but hearing your own name can also give you feel-good hormones, just like kindness. It is said that saying someone's name can cause unconscious signals such as empathy, trust, and compassion to the unconscious brain. So why not say their name; it could make their day even better.
~ https://www.hustlefromtheheart.com/blog/names

5. **Send birthday cards**.

What? No, not a Facebook message or a text. I'm talking about a handwritten greeting, and mailing it. Yes! You can get a box of 16 cards from Half Priced Books for less than $4.00. You can order stamps and have them sent to you. It's so easy.

Who doesn't love mail, especially if they are not bills or solicitations? Mailing a card just takes a couple minutes to sign and address. It's an effective way to make someone's day the good old fashion way.

6. **Send a text or make a phone call, just because**.

How often do you think of an old friend or family member who you haven't seen or talked to in a while? This thought usually occurs at a random time, when you can't always reach out to them, but make a note. Start a list. Write their name or record a voice memo on your phone to remind yourself to reach out to them. It doesn't have to be much, maybe just a quick text: "I'm thinking of you and hope you are doing well," or if you can, be specific: "I just drove past the ice cream shop where we last met. 'Hope we can do that again soon."

I did this just recently with a former coworker and he replied, "You made my day!" Mission accomplished! I can cross that off my list and then I was clear for the day.

7. **Do something nice for your family**.

Sometimes it's easier to give to strangers than it is your own family. We tend to take family for granted or let them drive us a little crazy, forgetting to let them know how much we love them. Maybe a note on the mirror, or in a lunch box. My teenagers hate it, but I think they secretly love it. Make their favorite dessert and with intent, put it on a plate, and let them know you made it with love. Pray over the dessert and your son or daughter, and pray that it fills them with love from above.

> ... pray that it fills them with love from above.

8. **Last, but definitely not least, make *your* day**.

If making another person's day hasn't made your day *yet*, or you have just had "one of those days," give yourself the gift of time, a gift of time with the Lord. Spend time with the Word, give yourself a prayer or blessing before you end the day. You can't make the day of others if your cup isn't full.

> You can't make the day of others if your cup isn't full.

You can probably tell I like lists. I make lists of lists that I need to make. I make lists for myself and for my family all the time. Here's my list for you:

1. Serve our Lord.
2. Serve each other.
3. Serve yourself.

In service, *God's promises* and presence come alive in your life and the lives of others. Scriptures guide us. Here are some of my favorites:

Romans 8:28:

And we know that in all things God works for the good of those who love him, who have been called according to his purpose.

Ephesians 6:7:

Serve wholeheartedly, as if you were serving the Lord, not people, ...

Proverbs 11:25 (ESVUK):

Whoever brings blessing will be enriched, and one who waters will himself be watered.
~ The Holy Bible, English Standard Version Copyright © 2001 by Crossway Bibles, a division of Good News Publishers.

Matthew 20:28 (CSB):

"… just as the Son of Man did not come to be served, but to serve, and to give his life as a ransom for many."

~ The Christian Standard Bible. Copyright © 2017 by Holman Bible Publishers. Used by permission. Christian Standard Bible®, and CSB® are federally registered trademarks of Holman Bible Publishers, all rights reserved.

Dear God, Thank You. Thank you for giving me the courage to interrupt someone's life with a smile or a loving act. Thank you for using me to reach people where they are, when they need it. Thank you for giving me the joy and filling my heart when someone smiles or tells me that I made their day.

Lord, please continue to use me in small ways that make big impact. Amen.

*****

Any Friend of Yours Is a Friend of Mine

From Janine:

The friends in our local church community are incredibly generous, following God's model of caring for one another. Often when a friend is in need, a message is sent to the local Christian community, requesting help. Whether it is prayer, donations, help around the house, running errands or meals, the community assists and supports each other. I like to help when I can, even if I don't know the person. If someone is a friend of our community of believers, then he or she is a friend of mine.

That's how I met Glen Aubrey. It was February, 2020, and I signed up to bring a meal to Glen, just like I have done for others. But this trip was special. Most often I drop off the meal and am on my way. But Glen invited me into his home. He shared some of his story with me and shared his library with me. We had such a great conversation that I forgot temporarily that I had to pick up my kids. Then before I left, he asked if he could play me a song. It was so moving and generous. I could tell he was playing for me, from his heart. I enjoyed every note.

Over the next few months, we developed a friendship that I am grateful for. I have such a strong respect and appreciation for his work and hobbies. I always leave his presence feeling better, inspired, and hopeful. He is just so encouraging and positive; he always makes my day.

And what do I do for a living? I am currently a Shopper Marketing Internal Consultant for a major consumer packaged food company and have been blessed by this company for more than twenty-three years. Although I am not native to Texas, I live in Fort Worth with my husband of almost twenty years and have two amazing teenagers who challenge me daily to be a better person.

~ Janine Cushman, July 2021

From Glen:

It has been a true privilege to observe God fulfilling His promises and examples of love through the life and testimony of Janine, her husband, Jim, and family. I am the recipient of their compassion, and their obedience to God's command: to love one another. One phrase immediately comes to mind: *"gracious giving."*

~ Glen Aubrey, July, 2021

*****

Carol's Story
Divine Faithfulness Amidst Human Suffering

Jack Elwood
Executive Director, Heal Africa USA

Genesis 50:20
You intended to harm me, but God intended it for good to
accomplish what is now being done,
the saving of many lives.

Romans 8:28
And we know that in all things God works for the good
of those who love him, who have been called according to
his purpose.

My life and the lives of my family were forever changed by a simple invitation that was made to my five-year-old sister, whom I never met. This invitation was for her to attend a Vacation Bible School. In the summer of 1954, my family moved to Renton, Washington, where my father was working for the government as an engineer. He was building a home by himself, and my mother and their three young daughters ages nine, seven, and five, were living in the basement as he worked evenings to build the main floor.

My parents were not religious at the time and obviously had a lot on their plates. When the neighbor next door offered to take the girls to a weeklong Vacation Bible School during the mornings, they thought it could not hurt.

My sisters came back each day quoting John 3:16 and singing "Jesus loves me, this I know ..." [Composed in 1859 by Anna Bartlett Warner, Public Domain]. My mother was pregnant at the time (with yours truly), and they had no idea how this would lay a foundation for generations to come, as their world was about to be rocked by devastating news.

Over the next few weeks, the youngest daughter, Carol, became quite sick. She was eventually diagnosed with leukemia and in a matter of six short weeks, she died. As she lay dying, she would sing those songs from Vacation Bible School, and quote John 3:16:

> For God so loved the world that he gave his
> one and only Son, that whoever believes in him
> shall not perish but have eternal life.

She would tell my parents, "Don't worry about me; I am going to be with Jesus ..." which today is inscribed on her tombstone.

The week after she died, my parents went to the church where the girls had learned of this Jesus and His love for us. The pastor and his wife led my parents to give their broken hearts to the Lord and the church rallied behind my family, helping them turning a growing house into a godly home. When I was born, they dedicated me to the Lord and to His work (like Samuel of old). They would go on to have two more sons. All five of their children would go on to grow as devoted followers of Christ and serve in ministry and missions.

Over 50 years later, as the president of a mission agency, I was invited to return to speak at this church and to thank them for their impact and to help commission missionaries from that church. Unbeknownst to me, sitting in the front row of the church, filled with hundreds of people, was an old woman (in her nineties). As I retold the story of my family, I could see her begin to weep. The pastor then came up and said: "That's the woman who invited your sisters to Vacation Bible School." You see, she had felt that for most of her life she had never accomplished anything for the Lord. After the service, I was able to tell her about how our family had grown in faith and that now each of my four children and their spouses and children were followers of Christ. Needless to say, there was not a dry eye in the house!

That very weekend I flew to Quito, Ecuador to meet with a group of dedicated missionaries. Our mission had been there for over one hundred years, and we were celebrating a work that had planted scores of churches among many different cultures and languages. In 1956, a group of five missionaries (Jim Elliot, Nate Saint, Roger Youderian,

Peter Fleming, and Ed McCulley) were martyred there in the jungles among the Auca people).
~ https://en.wikipedia.org› wiki › Jim_Elliot

That tragic event has been the most catalytic event in modern mission history over the last 100 years. It has probably propelled hundreds, if not thousands of people to serve Christ, cross culturally.

The lesson again was that God uses tragic, painful, even mortal events for good, if we trust Him. It does not mean God is the author of evil or that He delights to harm those He loves. It simply means He uses pain for good (Romans 8:28) even when we cannot see the short-term benefits or understand the long-term impact. It also does not mean we will always see the direct correlation between our suffering and our good, but it does mean **we can trust God and His promises**. Like a coach who pushes athletes in practice, in the weight room, and in the game itself, God uses all of life to help us discover that He is more than able to help us grow in grace, faith, and maturity.

> We can trust God and His promises.

I would experience the reality of the principle only a few hours later in Ecuador when I received a frantic call from my wife, saying that my daughter's boyfriend (soon to be fiancée) had just died in a tragic fall while hiking with some friends.

He had hopes of being a missionary in Africa and was my daughter's first boyfriend.

I had told my staff earlier in the year that the weakness in my human armor was my daughter. I have three amazing sons whom I love and respect but there is something special about a dad and a daughter's relationship. She is the "apple of my eye" and I was devastated for her. I was able to finally get a return flight back to the U.S., just in time for the funeral and saw her publicly share about God's grace at the funeral service.

I was the missionary, pastor, and mission executive who usually presided over events like this, but I was being held up by my wife, Joan, as I was overcome with emotions I had never experienced before. It was raw, it was real, and it was hard to understand. I discovered that truth understood intellectually was one thing while truth understood experientially is another.

> I discovered that truth understood intellectually
> was one thing
> while truth understood experientially is another.

I cannot tie a nice, neat little bow on the lesson and flippantly claim to know the "whys" of such a tragic death. I do know the promises of God are true and that is enough for me. C. S. Lewis once said: "But pain insists upon being attended to. God whispers to us in our pleasures, speaks in our conscience, but shouts in our pains: it is his megaphone to rouse a deaf world."

~ C. S. Lewis, *The Problem of Pain* (1940; repr., San Francisco: Harper San Francisco, 2001), 14.

When we understand that faith does not insulate us from a life of pain and suffering, we discover that God empowers us to live through the challenges of living in a fallen, sinful world, knowing He is with us and promises to redeem it for our good and his glory. It is our submission to His sovereignty that enables us to live with His promises as sufficient for the hour; at least that truth is what I have discovered so far.

> It is our submission to His sovereignty that enables us to live with His promises as sufficient for the hour ...

*****

From Jack:

[Dr. Jack Elwood is husband of one, a father of four, and a grandfather of nine. He currently serves as the Executive Director of Heal Africa USA. He has served as a missionary to Taiwan with the Navigators, a pastor to four churches, and the president of Avant Ministries.

He currently resides with his wife, Joan, in Round Hill, Virginia. Contact Dr. Jack Elwood: jackelwood@gmail.com]

Glen Aubrey and I met in 1976 at Faith Chapel in San Diego, California, where he was serving as the worship leader. He later contributed his musical talents at our wedding. He has been a lifetime friend and invaluable ministry consultant in two different churches where I served as Senior Pastor. Glen is one of the most talented and gifted individuals I have had the privilege of serving with in the Kingdom.

~ Jack Elwood, July, 2021

From Glen:

Serving with Jack Elwood through two church consultation arrangements, long after his wedding to Joan, was a great privilege. Jack and I share identical spiritual philosophies, grounded in knowing God's will. I was (and am) humbled with his missionary heart and his compassion to reach the world. We also shared a lot of humor, which we both needed at times. Jack, you are a true servant of our Lord.

~ Glen Aubrey, July, 2021

God — A Part of Everyday Life

Richard (Rick) Fleming

Author: *Living Faith * Inspiring Stories to Encourage You*
This book is currently in development.
To be published by Creative Team Publishing
www.creativeteampublishing.com.

The Desert Adventure

I was raised in a family who went to church every time the doors were open. I attended a Christian school through the eighth grade. Every night, I went to sleep knowing that my parents and grandparents prayed for me by name. Their prayers were for God's hand to protect and guide me. I got used to God being a part of my everyday life nearly from the beginning.

We were a family that spent most of our free time outside. Two younger brothers, mom, dad, and I spent time at the beach, camping, hunting, or fishing. As I got older, target practice became my favorite stress reliever. My favorite safe place to enjoy this pastime was in the El Centro desert, in Southern California. I invited a friend to join me one sunny summer day.

We drove in my truck to the area that I usually went to, and there were people close by, so that location would not work. We went exploring to find another area that would be safe and serve our needs.

Reaching an unfamiliar area, I ended up driving into a patch of loose sand. There was no choice but to stop. We were stuck. We tried several methods to get free, but none of them worked. We had plenty of water, snacks, and protective clothing and were prepared for the 112-degree weather.

We gathered up our supplies and the guns, and walked several miles to Interstate 8. Arriving on the side of the freeway, we started thumbing for a ride. The weather was extremely hot, and the nearest shade was at least half a mile, or more, away. We were losing a lot of fluid in sweat, but walking in the desert toward the shade was our only option.

Imagine this picture: two young, rough looking characters carrying several guns, including rifles and pistols, hoping someone would stop and give them a ride. Well, there was not much of a chance any driver would accommodate. And none did.

We had walked down the Interstate for a while when a California Highway Patrol (CHP) officer stopped to check on us. We put our guns down so he would know we were of no threat.

The officer was at the end of his shift, but he picked us up and drove us to a restaurant in El Centro, about fifteen miles away, where we cooled off and continued to hydrate. When we had recovered from the heat, the officer, now off the clock, drove to the CHP garage. He picked up a 4-wheel drive vehicle, returned to the restaurant, retrieved us, and drove us to my truck. He had set his gun belt down on his seat while he worked the winch, and eventually pulled us out of the sand. We both felt that his rescuing included a lot of trust as well as provision.

God promises He will never forsake us. See Hebrews 13:5b: "… God has said, 'Never will I leave you; never will I forsake you.'" God provided us with the right person at the right time, who had access to the equipment needed at that moment. He was a gift, one example of God being a part of everyday life and of fulfilling His promises to care for His children.

Marriage, a Redemption, and the Love of My Life

One fall day in 1982, I was invited by a friend, who also was a choir director, to sing in his choir for a Christmas musical. At my first rehearsal with the choir, because of an overfull schedule, I was a few minutes late arriving, and then had to leave early for an appointment.

I am afraid I did not make a very good first impression!

However, I sat next to an attractive soprano who had a wonderful high voice. The next day I asked the director, "Who was the young lady I sat next to? Did you know she can sing very high?" The director responded that he did not know who she was; she was so quiet. Well, I found out later her name was Patti. The very next practice the director gave her a high note and she nailed it.

We Missed Each Other Numerous Times, but God Fulfilled His Promise: We Met on *His* Timing!

As Patti and I got to know each other better, we learned that our paths had been crossing for years. In fact, when she was born, her family lived two blocks from my family, and I walked past her house every day when I walked to school. I sang with a group at her church, twice. Both times she had experienced work conflicts and was not there.

I left a job in October of 1979, and she started at the same place of employment in November. Missed again! There were several other times, too, beyond these incidents where we just missed each other. In God's timing, however, we went on our first date in December 1982, got engaged the last day of January 1983, and got married that next August.

Two years later I received a job opportunity that required a move to Tennessee. We prayed about it in October, visited the site in November, and moved in January: definitely God's timing for both Patti and I.

That was 38 years ago! My wife and I now have two grown boys. And the blessings were not concluded: God added a terrific Christian daughter-in-law and grandson to the mix.

It's true: We have seen God's guiding hand leading us from the moment we met, through courtship, the move to Tennessee, job changes, children, church work, and a health scare or two.

He has always been faithful; He has never let us down.

Everything Was Going Well with My Career, and Then ...

After sixteen years in a safety job that had grown up around me, achieving safety numbers that were very good, with numbers of accidents down, everything appeared to be going well. Imagine my surprise when I was let go.

My first thought was, "God, what are your plans for us now? I'm an over-60-year-old man and not ready to retire. What kinds of jobs are out there?" I immediately started sending out resumes and reaching out to my network of business associates, but with no responses.

A friend from the church choir suggested I look into an opportunity he had heard about, and I did. Long weeks went by. Then I got an email with a few questions. Finally, progress, praise the Lord. More waiting, then an interview!

Patti, my wife, and I prayed for Gods will—and a job. I worried about my full beard; I thought that some would consider it to be not businesslike enough. I arrived at the location and met the interviewer, and when he turned around, he had a beard four times the size of mine.

My thought was this: "Relax. God's got this." During the interview we were joined by the beard's boss and the three of us started talking like old friends. There was laughter, detailed questions, a scripture quoted, and I left, comfortable with everything.

On the way home I told Patti that I wanted the job before I even knew the benefits package. I was satisfied; I believed this company and position were exactly right for me. This was where I wanted to work. I was convinced: God had prepared this opportunity for me.

I started work weeks later and it was everything I had hoped for. The man I worked next to was a Christian who would, out of the blue, quote a scripture, ask a Bible question, or sing a hymn. Yes, it was also more money, fewer hours, and far less stress.

After a few weeks, each of my sons separately commented, "Dad, you are going to live longer with that job." As of this writing, I have been here three years and continue grow in the position.

Once again, God had taken me out of my comfort zone, though it was a poor situation, and moved me into a much better one. He was faithful and upheld His promises to me.

> … God took me out of my comfort zone, even though it was a poor situation, and moved me into a much better one. He was faithful and upheld His promises to me.

*****

From Rick:

I first met Glen when he became the Music Director for the choir at Faith Chapel, La Mesa, California. I was used to directors who were older, so I was surprised to see that he was so young. His obvious talent and personality quickly won me and the rest of the choir over.

For our first one-on-one rehearsal, I went to his office and found him at his desk writing a song. Using the desk, he moved his fingers as if playing the piano, hearing the chords in his mind as he did, and then noting the music on a leadsheet. I was impressed to say the least.

That was the start of a long-lasting friendship. Following the church choir experience, we worked together in the Youth for Christ, San Diego (YFC) performing group, *Masterpeace* and became even better friends. Much later, Glen (along with Cindy, his wife, and their two children, Heather and Justin) visited us in Tennessee. Glen was working with my church, as a part of his consultation services with local churches, one of which was mine. Every time the goal and activities of his engagements were devoted to helping improve a church's programing and worship services.

Time passed. We have been friends through weddings, children born and raised, each moving to new states, and now we both have grandchildren. We have been good friends for over 45 years.

Very few people enjoy that kind of friendship. I am blessed.

~ Rick Fleming, August, 2021

From Glen:

It was a true pleasure to enjoy Rick's presence and singing ability in the Faith Chapel church choir in the late 1970s. His tenor voice was professional and inspirational; he sounded great and read music, too! Afterward, he joined our San Diego Youth for Christ singing group, *Masterpeace,* the first edition.

This group performed in many local San Diego churches for several years.

One marked highlight of our friendship was getting to know Rick's family after he married Patti. Her father, Jack Armstrong, became a model and mentor to me for years. In fact, I was honored to receive permission from the family to tell his story in *Industrial Strength Solutions * Build Successful Work Teams*, beginning on page 55. (This book is available through Barnes and Noble, at this website: **https://www.barnesandnoble.com/w/industrial-strength-solutions-glen-aubrey/1111674870**.)

The story is worth relating here, as an example of God's provision and fulfillment. A special word of thanks to Kathy Armstrong, his wife, for the permission to print this story. Jack was **The Teacher** in countless ways. He was a fulfillment of one of God's promises to me, his family, and others of the Christian community, demonstrating and teaching through his example, traits of Godly character. Here is a summary of one remarkable encounter:

The Teacher

Jack was a friend, a gentleman much older than I. He was a WWII Veteran, having fought in battles I had only read about. I am a baby-boomer, so WWII and the events surrounding it would always be a study for me and not a lived experience. Yet, somehow, as on occasion I had opportunity to view Jack, watch him work, and hear his philosophical pronouncements, I was given opportunity to "live" in his experiences as I sought to learn from the life lessons he taught, and there were many.

He was a tradesman. After the War's conclusion he decided to settle, start a family, and chose what was to become my neck of the woods as his domicile. I first met him in a non-profit charitable organization where he won me over with his smile and accent—decidedly Southern, and genuine. His interest in me, I have concluded since, did not originate in shared abilities—we were very different from one another. Rather, it originated in our mutual understanding of service with quality behind the scenes—we mutually tried to contribute with excellence whether anyone noticed or not. Our hidden-from-the-applause efforts were those we didn't speak about; somehow talking about or dwelling too much on what we had done could, or would, sacrifice the purity of any good or best motive in the earnest methods of an endeavor, if not the endeavor itself. Accenting humility would somehow cause that humility to lose its full impact and become not so humble any more. So, we both just "knew."

Jack helped me, and I helped him to the extent that I could, and I always admired his diligence and desire to serve. His trade was that of electrician. I was one of those who knew enough about electricity to leave it alone, and by the time I met Jack I had already fried at least one screwdriver. Clearly this was a field in which I should walk as an observer and only at a distance. During this time we developed several electrical installation needs at our home, so I asked Jack if he would come and do the work, fully intending to pay him what I would have paid any other electrician.

Jack was always on time. I struggled in this area. He showed me the value of commitment, through his example, and I learned and tried to put his model into practice. I watched him work. I saw him struggle. I saw him get hurt while climbing over beams to run wire. Remember, he was a WWII Veteran, and this was the 1980's. He was "old" by my age standards, and I wanted to make sure he didn't slip or fall. However, watching him and hearing him, I realized I was the one who would slip and fall before he ever would … in principles, character, right standing, and commitments. So we both hung on.

One particular day in what was turning out to be a "larger than expected" wiring job for which I was "hiring" him (he refused payment at the end) he was embattled mightily with a wire run that would have challenged anyone regardless of age or ability. It was a hot day, oppressively so, and Jack was sweating like a shower. I wanted to help, and while telling him of my intentions, and trying to lend a hand there was no way I could really be of any significant assistance — there was room for only one where he was sandwiched — so I mainly tried to keep out of the way, steady the ladder, and offer him cold drinks when he would come down and shake off the dust. At one point in his efforts while aloft in the crawl space, and probably not aware I could hear him, he made a comment I will forever remember. It was this, addressed with intent and firm commitment to the wire with which he was having so much trouble, inconvenience and discomfiture: "I'm gonna win — I'm gonna win." And in due time, he did, yes, did he ever. That installation, his installation, remains well into the 2000's and needs no improvement.

Years passed. Jack and his family moved to the Deep South. He had retired and wanted to go to the place of his roots. One of the peculiar incidents of life then occurred, a juxtaposition of people, places, and times that upon review and contemplation contribute to cherished memories. I was invited to be the speaker at a series of training sessions for his son-in-law (Rick Fleming), one of my dearest friends. Upon accepting the invitation, I asked if Jack might attend any of the sessions — it would be good to see him. You see, in the intervening years he had contracted cancer, and while never forfeiting his optimism, he was suffering and all knew that the battle would draw to a close in time.

It was a special and tender moment when, after one seminar, Jack came up to speak to me. I had seen him in the audience, and my countenance must have alluded to the fact that I was glad he was there, because I was, sincerely. When we met in person down front we greeted each other warmly. The same deep respect I had felt so many years before seemed even more a gift I desired to give back. This was a great man who at this time was physically struggling, and bearing his condition well. We spoke of his disease and I asked him how he was doing. Without reservation he described the pain, but through his confident comments he made it clear that he had decided his discomfort was not going to be his focus ... unbelievably, his focus was centered on me. Out of high regard I ventured only as far as I thought appropriate in discussing his health and prognosis. At one point, he seemed to let down a bit ... and ventured comments, describing that the cancer was getting him, and he knew it.

It was a poignant moment. I said, "Jack ... let me remind you of something that may encourage you." I reminded him about the wiring job, the difficulty, the stress of the installation, the commitment he showed and his outstanding positive attitude.

He remembered. Then I said, "Jack, when the job was so tough that most men would have cursed it and the guy who hired them, you addressed the wire." He looked puzzled. "You spoke to the wire," I stated it differently, and some of the confusion in his face dissolved. "Jack," I said, "Remember what you said? You said: 'I'm gonna win, I'm gonna win.' And you did!"

His understanding was greater than mine. I sought conclusion but his was already enveloping my next comment: "In this current challenge, my friend, remember what you said. You will win ... you will win." Eyes glistened, tears followed, we gave each other a hug, and we parted.

It was several months later when Jack died. But clearly, he had won. He had shown a younger friend who needed the lesson and the encouragement how to win in difficult times and uncomfortable circumstances, and had taken it upon himself to win again, no matter the odds. His win is seen in the strong legacy he left — in his family, his extended family, and one friend who is older now, who watched him work on a hot day with a challenging electrical installation where character and fortitude were evidenced in strong measure, and resiliency of character won the day. Jack, you were then, and are now, a true inspiration. You, sir, are a winner.

We recognize God's provisional strength for us in others. May that recognition become our motivation and inspiration to be thankful and to give unto others. In doing so, we honor God, His presence, and promises well.

~ Glen Aubrey, August, 2021

*****

God's Sustaining Grace

Robert Glenn
Author: *Rearing Up America * The Journal of a Father's Reflection on Special Needs*
Published by Creative Team Publishing
www.creativeteampublishing.com © 2012

Wow: What has God done for me? Maybe a better question is: What hasn't He done? After all, He walks with me on a daily basis. What more can one ask from a true friend, let alone from our Creator? Have you found this "true friend"? If not, how could you begin the search?

To start with, one should understand that God does need to be counted as your personal friend. And the only way to know someone is to become introduced. There are two ways; the first is to be introduced by a mutual friend and secondly, through reading the Bible on your own. Both work but the bottom line is, the choice is up to you. After hearing about Gods' true love for you and the ultimate sacrifice His Son, Jesus, made for us all, we (you) must be the one(s) to declare, "I believe. I believe You died for me, and I accept your gift of love."

In doing so, your friendship begins as well as a brand-new journey in life. The journey will truly have no end. It is a true friendship you can always count on. The Bible tells us in 1 Corinthians 2:10-16 that as a result of our belief, His Spirit comes to dwell within us, in the being of the Holy Spirit, and will teach us many things.

"God living in us." This is a stumbling block for many. But having faith is totally different from having knowledge. We are never promised all knowledge, but God does promise to never leave or forsake us, no matter what. I value that promise far above any earthly promise.

> … God does promise to never leave or forsake us, no matter what.

You and I should soon learn to let God be God, and trust in His ability to care for His children. He will reveal that which we need to know, and no more. This assurance provides comfort and peace of mind.

You see, man was given a mind to exercise free choice and as we all know, man doesn't always choose wisely. This world will always be full of challenges, but once we have a relationship with a true friend, Jesus, we have all we need to meet any challenge head-on.

So, what about me? What have my challenges been? What has God done for me and why do I trust Him? How do I experience the presence of His love every day?

Well, trying to convey the magnitude of my family's journey is going to be a real challenge for me to relate in this one chapter. I have written two books on this topic and a set of lecture notes. I have become not only an advocate for our daughter, who has a very rare genetic disorder, but for all individuals who live with any rare condition.

I must begin by saying I do not believe God *causes* bad things to happen to us. He does, however, transform the bad results of those experiences into good, which only He can do.

I used to ask the question, "Why?" on a regular basis, out of the emotional pain I felt and the physical pain our daughter, Joy, was living with. Why should a small child go through such a hard life experience? That questioning phase has now passed even though I will not have a full understanding in my lifetime.

I now have a growing trust in God, which has evolved from seeing His work in our lives for thirty-four years. Trust is a daily occurrence, in which I consciously place my choices. These are not only choices about what I should do or say, but also about how I should feel.

How trust works in the relational aspects of the relationship between God and man: I believe God gives love, peace, assurance, and healing, but not at our beckoned call. Trust, on our part is essential and must be pursued, regardless of circumstances.

Let me explain the reality of God's love by beginning to share with you some of our family's story. My wife, Lee, and I have two children. Our daughter, Joy, was born with an extremely rare genetic brain disorder called Lissencephaly (literally translated — smooth brain). The condition is also known as Double Cortex or Subcortical Band Heterotopia.

For the first twelve years of her life, Joy's main diagnosis was CP (Cerebral Palsy), partially due to available medical technology used to identify the actual diagnosis. For the first eight years of her life, Joy demonstrated significant challenges with both gross and fine motor skills, including eating and speech. Her cognitive level held fast at around a two-year-old level.

Joy was unable to bathe or dress herself because her motor skills were so compromised. She was unable to push a button through a buttonhole or work a zipper. Her vocabulary consisted of about 100 words and these were spoken in single words or short phrases. Joy did have a wonderful bright personality and loved to smile. Her laugh was absolutely contagious.

Perhaps you can already imagine that child-care was involved (time consuming). After eight years, however, we had a handle on the routine and were already trusting God for the strength, peace, hope; and for the perseverance we would need for the years ahead.

Even though I didn't know why this condition was happening to our daughter, I did have peace. With God's help we knew we would be fine. Honestly, those feelings back then were perhaps driven more from my human nature than complete dependence on God. I'll explain this last thought in more detail later on.

Lee and I were praying back then and felt God's answers for our daily needs, but one day those needs soared to new heights. God knew the true reality of Joy's condition and, in His wisdom, He had been equipping us for the days to come.

One afternoon while sitting at the kitchen table at snack-time, Joy had a small seizure. From that day and for the next four years, she had seizures every day. Literally, every day they grew in number and strength. Joy was placed on anticonvulsants, but in eighteen (short/long) months, the seizures had grown stronger, and she was having eighty or more seizures every day. This level of seizure activity continued on for two and a half years. We believed we were losing her.

By the time we were about four years into her seizure activity, our happy little girl could no longer laugh, speak, or even form a smile. I would ask Joy if she could give Pop a smile; and all she was able to do was to slightly raise the corners of her mouth and then her lips would quickly flatten-out. I was heart-broken at the swift and continuing decline of her health.

It was during this period of time that our hearts and minds truly sought God's help, and we felt Him truly at our side. It wasn't a daily or even hourly relationship with God then; it was literally a moment-by-moment dependence. I had learned just what it means to "pray unceasingly." He carried us through each day; one day-at-a-time.

I mentioned earlier in this chapter that once we believe, God's Holy Spirit comes to dwell in us. He does! All good things come from God. God gives good things to everyone (whether one believes in Him or not), but a huge change in understanding occurs once a person puts their life into God's care. As a believer, you and I recognize the Source of goodness. Non-believers can live their entire lives and believe good things just happen, often expressing, "I have a good life; why do I need God?"

That question has become a stumbling block for many people. The more important question which is often not asked is this: "Why do I even need a personal relationship with God?" Ones who ask this often do not even consider the Creator who made man, and who desires His creation to come back to Him and have a personal relationship with Him.

God loves you so much! Thank goodness Lee and I know this truth. You can know it, too.

> God loves you so much! Thank goodness Lee and I know
> this truth.
> You can know it, too.

During our rough periods, God carried us and Joy through unimaginable days and months. Along with Joy's daily seizures, she was also experiencing some Grand Mal seizures. Often a Grand Mal seizure stood as a single seizure event, but on two occasions in an eighteen-month span, the Grand Mal seizures clustered for three straight hours. I simply can't describe the emotions which swelled up inside of me on those occasions. All we could do was to hold Joy in our arms and wait it out.

The doctors would instruct us to give Joy an extra dose of meds during these extended periods of seizure clusters, however they never suggested the ER (Emergency Room) as an option. They knew all the ER could do was to also provide additional meds. We knew no other infections were causing the problem; Joy was constantly monitored. The medical community did what they could, but frankly, they didn't know how to help her.

At this point I will share some general information to set the groundwork for our journey's path. I begin by defining what identifies a condition as being a rare disorder. Generally, a disorder is defined as rare when there are 200,000 or less individuals affected on a global scale. To date, there are about

7,000 conditions labeled as rare, and more than 90% of them do not have an FDA approved Treatment Plan (according to NORD – The National Organization for Rare Diseases).

So, even though an individual has a rare disorder, they may also have a number of treatable conditions which do have FDA approved treatment programs: i.e., Epilepsy. Issues may evolve when these treatable conditions are addressed by using the same FDA treatment plans established for the normal population, with no consideration given to the patients' untreatable main diagnosis.

It is generally understood different people react differently to medication treatments. One unknown factor may be addressed with the following question: "To what extent does a rare disorder exacerbate or complicate a medication's intended benefit?" It's an interesting thought; it may take a considerable amount of time to delve into this issue, time which many doctors simply may not have.

Advocacy is needed. And it was this very question which fueled my desire to do research on behalf of our daughter and all those individuals who may be affected.

Advocacy is needed. And it was this very question which fueled my desire to do research on behalf of our daughter and all those individuals who may be affected.

If you have a child with an extremely rare disorder, even though you are seeing a specialist for a known condition (say it's Epilepsy), the doctor may have never had a patient with your child's main diagnosis before in their practice. Remember, a rare disorder is one affecting 200,000 people or less; there are currently 3.4 million people treated for Epilepsy in the USA alone (globally about 50 million). Epilepsy is not a rare disorder.

I encourage everyone to become a life-long learner; learning certainly does not end with a college degree. Learning is a gift (a skill) from God and should be revered as such.

Here is some basic information on Lissencephaly I used as a foundation to expand my understanding of our daughter's condition.

Lissencephaly is divided into 6 levels of severity (levels 1-5 have a life expectancy of up to 20 years, in a best-case scenario). Joy was placed in level 6, and level 6 is thought not to affect life expectancy, but I have only heard of one individual known to be in his forties. Still, Level 6 is the mildest and the rarest form of Lissencephaly.

To help explain this last point, here is a quick Doctoral Thesis in a peanut shell. Classic Lissencephaly is found in levels one through five. These individuals have one Cortex, as do all healthy brains, but the Cortex is unusually smooth and there is a smooth-variance through-out these five levels.

Then we have level 6; although still part of the Lissencephaly family, there is one distinct difference which sets it apart. Level 6 individuals have not one but two Cortexes, slightly separated by white (brain) matter and thus form an unusually thick Cortex (both Cortexes are also smooth in nature). This condition is only shared by about 200 individuals, globally.

Joy's brain needs a lengthy time to process any response. In short, this condition greatly impedes the brain's ability to communicate with its own body.

Epilepsy generally emerges in the first ten years of life. Joy came down with epilepsy as she was turning nine years old. She is now 34 years of age and, as of 2020, entering her twenty-fifth year of seizure activity. Her cognitive level at age 34 is about that of an autistic two-year-old and with this said, she is considered to be a genius for her diagnosis; this opinion was shared by Dr. William Dobyns (who headed up a Genetic Research Team on Lissencephaly). In contrast, the individuals living in the Lissencephaly level categories of 1 through 5 may only reach a cognitive level of three to five months of age.

Now it is easy to think back and say we should have asked a whole array of questions a few years prior, but simply making it through each day was our number one challenge and energy drainer.

In the first four-year period of Joy's seizure activity, we logged 84 new medication scripts, mostly aimed at futile attempts to control the horrible side effects of the medication. Seizure control was not on our daily radar screen back then.

You see, Joy has been challenged from the day she was born. Epilepsy was not her main or only diagnosis. Epilepsy was a result from … "What?" At that point in time, we did not know. Her main diagnosis back then was Cerebral Palsy, given to her so that she would be covered for the OT (Occupational Therapy), PT (Physical Therapy), and speech therapies she needed at an early age.

By the age of twelve, we were fearing for our daughter's life. We asked about alternative treatments (surgery). We started with the VNS (Vagal Nerve Stimulator), but it, like the medication, had no impact on the seizures. Even after the VNS surgery, Joy was still visibly worsening on a monthly basis.

Note, however: This was the point in time during the late summer of 1999 that Joy was given an MRI which uncovered her main diagnosis of Lissencephaly.

Seeing no improvements from the VNS surgery, Joy's doctor said the only other surgery might be brain surgery (a Corpus-Callosotomy). Then only four years into the Epilepsy diagnosis, Joy had that surgery in which the doctor cut all the nerves which pass through the Corpus Callosum, separating the two sides of the brain neurologically.

This was Joy's first miracle; when she woke up, her cognitive skills (speech, laughter, smiles, eating) instantly returned (*instantly*) to the level she enjoyed four years prior, and Joy was 100% seizure free. It was amazing. This event marked a new beginning for her.

However, Joy only enjoyed five weeks being seizure free and then other types of seizures emerged and continued to strengthen for the next seventeen years. During that period, the only tool we had was medication. With her new clean seizure slate, seizures then worsened on an annual basis instead of monthly, and the amount of medication seemed to parallel the increase of seizure activity.

Hindsight is more than a regrettable memory; it is a valuable evaluation tool with immense value. If one sees only failure in dredging up the past; think again. Failures are wonderful learning tools and vital components towards future successes. Now, many years after Joy's brain surgery, I realize Joy would have passed-away over fifteen years ago if it had not been for the Corpus-Callosotomy procedure.

> Hindsight is more than a regrettable memory; it is
> a valuable evaluation tool with immense value …
> Failures are wonderful learning tools and vital
> components towards future successes.

Joy's brain couldn't have sustained the mounting deterioration she had experienced during those first four years of seizure activity, for more than two or three more years. Even though the surgery's success was short lived; it gave us valuable information and comfort we could build upon.

Because Joy's condition has no cure, quality of life has always been on my mind; our daughter was once happy in her youth. We asked, "Will she ever be happy again?" As the strength and number of seizures grew after her brain surgery, her skill levels and ability to express happiness again began to fade.

Joy was twenty-one years into the Epilepsy by 2016 and the prevailing thought held by all was that her Epilepsy was degenerative (not a hopeful thought, is it?). No medication had even stabilized her condition and there were no other surgeries on the table we might use. Joy was still on four medications and getting worse.

Joy's Neurologist decided to remove one low-dose med due to ill side-effects and put her on the drug, Banzel. In four months, Joy was up to 2,100 mg per day which added to her other meds was the highest med level she had been on. After a short while, her food consumption decreased greatly. One might think the Banzel suppressed her appetite (it's a common side-effect), but actually that was not the case.

Joy's fine motor skills had hit rock bottom. It was taking her about three minutes of actively attempting to open her mouth (I call it smacking her lips together) in order for her to take in one teaspoon of food. She wanted to eat but could not. Mealtime was easily an hour long just to help her eat a small portion of food. It seemed sometimes like we were feeding an injured baby bird.

Joy was living at an Intermediate Care Facility (ICF) by then because we could not provide the level of care she needed at home. We noticed she was losing weight, so I asked nursing how much she weighed. After only ten months on the Banzel, Joy had lost twenty-four pounds. I knew right away we needed to lower her Banzel to a level in which her motor planning skills might be restored, and she could eat on her own. We felt this was certainly a quality-of-life issue.

The doctor, however, was not happy about this, stating Joy's seizure activity would certainly go up. But we insisted, and he relinquished; the med reduction began. In another ten months, Joy went down from the 2100 to 600 mg per day, but her motor planning had not improved (an unforeseen outcome to say the least.)

However, my wife and I felt like we were seeing fewer seizures (or so it seemed), and Joy's care givers also noticed it. The ICF keeps an electronic record of seizure activity, so I asked for a copy. The analysis revealed that Joy's documented seizure activity went down 40% in that same ten-month period. This was the first time we had observed, as well as had documented proof, that Joy's seizures were not degenerative. This knowledge in retrospect was her second miracle.

Okay, now things actually got more complicated, but I will condense things down for time's sake. The medication levels continued to go down and up, because the doctors would not acknowledge the benefit Joy was experiencing on a lower dose, even-though they read the same seizure reports we had. Each time the meds were raised, Joy's seizure counts also went up and behaviors went south. Each time the meds were lowered, she would get better. Talk about the proverbial chicken and egg controversy!?

I can only speculate: lowering medications to better control seizures is one of those "out-of-the-box" approaches usually not to be considered. "In the box" doctors generally medicate until an individual is stabilized or seizures are totally under control (makes good sense, doesn't it?). However, FDA (Food and Drug Administration) and CDC (Centers for Disease Control) recommendations are based on test groups and the results thereof which I suspect are run mainly with individuals having "normal brain function" (how else could one reliably publish useable test results?).

Well, our drive and earnest desire at that point in time was to take Joy off the last 600mg of Banzel, but the doctor refused. He recommended the University of Pittsburgh Medical Center, Epilepsy Center which is located in the nearby city of Oakland, Pennsylvania, and a new doctor was then on the case. Joy had not had an EEG (Electroencephalogram) in many years, so a lengthy EEG was ordered. The new doctor requested a five-day test (that would be a challenge for anyone without a short attention span); Joy managed to comply for 57 hours, and she was done; the test was over. However, the doctor in charge of the test was so concerned by the constant underlying seizure activity through-out the test, she immediately, at checkout, wanted to raise Joy's med level.

I disagreed, mentioning I was not surprised at the test results we saw, and if we could have compared this test to one taken a year ago, that test would have been 40% worse. The doctor could not grasp this concept. She was focused solely on that which was in front of her. Parents have a unique advantage in knowing the patient's full medical history, firsthand, which does express reality better than a medical chart, in my experience. We will all experience the highs and the lows of life. Remember through it all, failure is an excellent teacher. If you sense something is not right, say something.

Parents have a unique advantage in knowing the patient's full medical history, firsthand, which does express reality better than a medical chart, in my experience.
We will all experience the highs and the lows of life.
Remember through it all, failure is an excellent teacher. If you sense something is not right, say something.

I have no idea how many times Joy has been on the same roller coaster with her meds; how many times do we need to see failed results before we know the process being used, doesn't work?

Well, the process of lowering the medications continued and it did have its good moments (which included numbers of days with no seizures recorded at all) and bad moments (including several trips to the ER for strong clusters of seizures). However, today, as of this writing, Joy is on the lowest medication level she has ever been on, and she has regained her ability to eat and enjoy food; she is happy, talking, smiling, and cooperative through her daily routine, and we are documenting far fewer seizures.

She has been at this more stable level since April of 2020. In the past, it was not uncommon to see one to two dozen seizures per day; in one of our latest monthly reports, only three seizures were recorded for that reporting period. We are encouraged; most of the months now log less than a dozen seizures. I can't tell you how much it warms my heart to see our daughter smiling and happy again.

A normal medication process for controlling seizure activity is designed to bring a normal brain, which is experiencing seizures, back to a normal stable brain function. It is not designed for an abnormal brain, but is still "the go to" procedure.

After all, isn't Epilepsy just Epilepsy? Ah, no. In my book, it's not necessarily a stand-alone issue for those with rare disorders. Epilepsy is *not* a condition which falls into the category of a rare disorder.

So, what is smooth brain? Determining the answer has been our challenge for 34 years. I'll expand a little here from my earlier comments. Here is one analogy: take a piece of aluminum foil and wad it up tightly into a small ball; then gently open it up. Can you visualize this? This would represent a normal cortex with lots of little peaks and valleys all over its surface; it is on this type of terrane that all our neurotransmitters flourish (we don't have millions of them, but we do have hundreds of thousands of neurotransmitters). This is how all information is transmitted in and out of our brains.

Now take the same open piece of foil and run it under a warm iron with 2 or 3 passes; you may still see all the same creases, but many of the peaks and valleys are gone; this represents smooth brain. Without the peaks and valleys on the Cortex, there is a significant decrease in neurotransmitters.

So how many less? Your guess is as good as mine. But here are two questions.

1. How many less neurotransmitters would it take to reduce the operation of a normal adult brain to that of an autistic two-year-old?
2. How many neurotransmitters might be found on the cortex, let's say, in a level 1 Lissencephaly individual who does not live long enough to leave the hospital after birth?

Questions such as these are food for thought.

You see, I'm not simply talking about intelligence; the brain, as you know, also sends out messages to the body intended to move your muscles: i.e., so your lungs will expand and contract (we know what would happen if the muscles stopped moving). The brain will also let your body know when it is time to use the bathroom and we know what happens when our body doesn't clearly get that message. You may learn more about this as you age.

The brain supports our body's ability to live. Do you get my point here? All treatments for rare disorders should only be guided by conventional treatment programs, not "locked" into them (especially for those 90% plus disorders with no FDA approved treatment plan). There is a world of difference between a patient with Heterotopia (a concussion) and a patient with Subcortical Band Heterotopia (smooth brain).

During the recent medication reduction process Joy went through, I asked our Neurologist how a drug (Onfi in this case) actually worked to accomplish its goal of seizure control, and he honestly replied that he didn't know. I was told, "That was a question you should ask your pharmacist." So, I did. The pharmacist turned his computer screen in my direction and typed in: "What is the mechanism for Onfi?"

Mechanism was a new word for me, as were over 50% of the words I saw on the screen. However, my eyes opened wide when I saw a few familiar words in the paragraph: "Onfi as well as the general group of benzodiazepines work through the neurological system." This is the very system which is greatly compromised in our daughter.

Perhaps this is why Joy had such difficulty with all the side-effects from the drugs, but no relief from the seizure activity. There are other families of drugs which work through sodium or calcium channels, which might have been alternative treatment plans. In retrospect, this question should have been asked years ago, and is certainly out of a parent's general thought process. Who could have known?

One additional question I asked our pharmacist on another visit was this: "Is there a way to compare the drugs which are measured in hundreds of milligrams with those relatively newer drugs which are measured one milligram at a time?" I was expecting an answer like a ten to one ratio or even twenty-five to one. But to my disappointment, he said no, that to date there was no mathematical formula to mix the two measurement systems of medication into one number, to know how much medication an individual is actually on. I have double-checked this finding with another pharmacist.

Two different measurement systems with no known connection? This sent up a red flag in my brain which is yet unresolved. These new drugs are very potent. Med-students, here is an excellent topic for a thesis — develop the formula and solve for X.

Knowing the total drug level has no direct implications concerning the success of the treatment-plan. Let me repeat that: Knowing the total drug level has no direct implications concerning the success of the treatment-plan (it just doesn't). However, knowing the total drug level has great implications if one is trying to minimize the drug's side-effects. Trying to control side-effects when using multiple anticonvulsants is in itself, unmanageable. And side-effects may be as devastating to an individual as the condition being treated. I have too many stories I might share some day to illustrate this point.

Over the last four years, we have successfully lowered Joy's medication level by about 55%, resulting in the lowering of her documented seizure activity by about 90%. Joy is experiencing a better quality of life than she has had for the past twenty-five years. It is sad for me to think that we may have mismanaged Joy's treatment plan for nearly twenty-five years, but it is still sadder for me to imagine using the original treatment approach, for the remainder of her life.

Remember, failures are excellent teaching tools, and expose wonderful learning opportunities. Please do not beat yourself up when you recall your past failures. Actually, all success is birthed from failure (be it your own or someone else's). Please do not forget or ignore failures; grow from them.

> ... all success is birthed from failure (be it your own or someone else's).
> Please do not forget or ignore failures; grow from them.

What have I learned throughout this journey? A number of things come to my mind, and here are three:

1. One important principal is this: <u>God's Word isn't for the accumulation of knowledge</u>. The Bible doesn't say to memorize His Word in order to repeat it upon demand. <u>He encourages us to hide it in our hearts so</u>

that when trials come, we may have His strength to face the challenges which come along, head on.

The mere accumulation of regurgitated knowledge may easily cross the line into the realm of vanity. However, if we apply God's Word on a daily basis, others may see God in us and ask, "Where does this unexplainable strength come from?"

I chose the chapter title, *God's Sustaining Grace* with great intent. It is God, Himself, who not only gives us grace; it is also God who enables us to receive His gift of grace. Remember, I mentioned God is the Creator of all good. When Joy was going through her darker days (and there were many of those), God was always there. His presence was the sustaining hope which carried Joy and the family through each day. How God worked leads me a second lesson I learned.

2. Our journey has helped me to focus more on His Holy Spirit. It is the one part of the Trinity which is the least talked about entity of God's person. Jesus asked His disciples to wait, and He would send them the Holy Spirit. The Holy Spirit would continue to teach and guide them in His absence. The Holy Spirit leads us to understand many things; not limited to that of love, joy, peace, patience, kindness, goodness, faithfulness, meekness, and self-control. (Galatians 5:22-23)

   I have never heard an audible word from God, but I do hear from Him through the Holy Spirit. Sometimes it is just a feeling (a feeling which is unexplainable through my own human nature). Other times it is a thought which comes to my mind: a thought which I have never had before which proves to be consistent with God's Word, and was just what was needed for the challenge before me. There have been several of these thoughts which come as the very first thought in the morning when I open my eyes. Is that a coincidence? I think not.

3. <u>I believe a strong lesson for me is the one of selflessness</u>. This is the willful desire to put others first. It doesn't mean I don't take care of my own needs, but I prioritize my daily life far differently now than I used to. Does that make sense to you? This concept was so profoundly drilled into me during those two-and-one-half years in which Joy had eighty seizures each and every day. I think you may know where my focus was concentrated.

I am, in fact, still learning. I truly feel that failures and challenges are instructors from God. Let's all be open to learning and applying the lessons we are taught, freely sharing with others. My desire to participate in this writing project is solely embedded in communicating with you.

My hope is that you might apply whatever is appropriate from our family's journey to your family's journey. Our family is not really special on any human scale, but we are deeply loved by our Creator. Our journey has no end.

Oh, I must reiterate: God loves you!

*****

From Robert:

Glen Aubrey and I met sometime in 2010, when I was already two years into writing my first book. I needed a Publisher and located Creative Team Publishing online (www.CreativeTeamPublishing.com). After only a few short emails and conversations on the telephone, I knew Glen would be a wonderful fit for collaboration on the release of *Rearing Up America*.

I was right; Glen was encouraging and supportive. He let me work at my own pace, which I'm sure stretched his patience. We have only met in person once which was over lunch on one of his book tours in Gettysburg, Pennsylvania.

He is not only a professional; he is a friend.

~ Robert Glenn, June, 2021

From Glen:

The writing journey Robert Glenn and I shared was a reflection of the trials, tests, quests for knowledge, and enduring Biblical truths and relationships he and his family experienced, as they sought answers for their daughter, Joy. I recall moments of caring so deeply while knowing, simply, that we *didn't* know what could be done. I am convinced that it was in those times with **God's Promises** of comfort, care, and compassion, as well as a growing familiarity with Him and His Word, which sustained this precious family. The truth for us: no matter how rare and difficult the circumstances and conditions might be, God is present. He speaks, we "listen," and earnestly desire to obey and honor Him and His Holy Spirit who is the Comforter. As we learn more, we become even more dedicated to His promise of grace, which sustains us through it all. Robert Glenn: I am truly proud to be your publisher of ***Rearing Up America * The Journal of a Father's Reflection on Special Needs.***

~ Glen Aubrey, June, 2021

*****

Robert Glenn has published two books through Amazon's Kindle Direct Publishing:

1. ***Thank You for Walking the Walk with Me***—a follow-up to **Rearing Up America**

2. ***Fishers of Men*** — a Christian fiction novel

You may contact Robert Glenn at this email address: rearingupamerica@gmail.com

*****

God's Power Is Promised To Pull Us Through Every Difficult Climb, and Overcome Every Stubborn Obstacle!

Pastor Vernon Lintvedt,
Blessed Savior Lutheran Church, O'Fallon, Illinois
Marty Lintvedt, Licensed Professional Counselor

God promises to never leave us or forsake us (Hebrews 13:5b).
He helps us as we trust in Him.
We believe that, because it is true.

Through Jesus, God's Power Pulls Us Through

This scripture comes to mind regarding a promise God made to us all: Hebrews 13:5b. In context, as we trust Him, "… God has said, 'Never will I leave you; never will I forsake you.'"

In summer, 2021, Blessed Savior Lutheran Church conducted a Vacation Bible School (VBS), for which I wrote the following article, an example of the resources, promises, and power of God.

I used and quoted from www.trains.com, and www.group.com, as follows:

> "Given a choice, railroads will always follow a straight, level path. Trains use less energy, speeds are higher, and there's less wear on equipment when railroads can build on an arrow-straight line. But the land rises and falls, obstacles must be avoided, and the ideal is more the exception than the rule."
> ~https://www.trains.com/trn/train-basics/abcs-of-railroading/grades-and-curves/ and
> ~https://www.group.com/category/ministry-resources/childrens-ministry/vbs/rocky-railway.do

Isn't that descriptive of our lives? In the journey of life when the path is straight and level, we're chugging along just fine. But, as the article says, "the ideal is more the exception than the rule." Can you relate?

What obstacles are stopping you from moving forward or slowing down your life, making it a steep and exhausting climb? Age? Maybe you're thinking about the day when running a marathon was not impossible with proper training. The power was there. But now you're standing at the bottom of a staircase hoping you can make it to the second floor. You look at your kids or grandkids and say, "If I could just bottle their energy, I would be a millionaire."

Maybe circumstances are slowing you down and you're running out of coal to run your life's engine. Your health takes a hit; an injury causing pain and frustration keeps you from focusing on and completing daily tasks; the workload at your job unexpectedly and suddenly increases bringing emotional and physical fatigue; the house or your car needs a major repair; the kids are needing more time and attention you don't seem to have; your marriage is struggling, negatively impacting every part of your life. These are just a few of the obstacles that slow us down or cause our internal engines to come to a complete halt.

The same thing can happen to a church. We're heading down the track and things are going smoothly and then COVID-19 hits. We think we're about to get to the end of that steep grade and then, the variant of that virus ramps up. Yet, the virus may be the smallest of obstacles the church has faced in recent years.

After WWII, churches were filled to capacity. The expression, "There are no atheists in the foxhole ..." drew people back to God and into the church. However, in the 1960s we began to see a subtle change. Our "enlightened" society began to believe that the power to make the world's locomotive smooth again was already inside us. We just needed to do more research and discover more technology, work smarter, and these actions will "solve all the problems we face as a society."

Consequently, the phrase, "Our help is in the name of the Lord ..." was no longer the axiom by which people used to live their lives and find hope. Look up the definition of the word axiom: "a statement or proposition which is regarded as being established, accepted, or self-evidently true."
~ [*Oxford Languages*]

When people know the real Truth, it guides and empowers their lives, when difficult climbs come, or we face seemingly unmovable obstacles. Sadly, technology hasn't become the little engine that could! Research and technology have certainly made many aspects of our lives easier and more comfortable, but when we look at our societal problems today, we cannot say we're improving.

Read the newspaper or listen to the news: does it feel like the world is calming down, or getting ready for Armageddon? In many ways our lives have become more lonely, more distrustful, more frustrating, and more powerless. In spite of all these steep climbs and unmovable obstacles of life, I believe there *is* power for us! Power to pull us through!

The theme for our VBS this year was "Jesus' Power Pulls Us Through." Jesus is the answer for us individually and as a Church. He is the power that can pull the world out of its misery today. Jesus' power has pulled many of us individually through some pretty steep climbs. Many have shared with me some life-threatening issues they have faced during this time and how they have found deliverance through faith and trust in Jesus' power. Seriously, we could fill an entire service with people testifying to Jesus' power at work in their lives. They are not just surviving, but thriving!

Many years ago, my wife, Marty, and I faced some physical challenges with a diagnosis of cancer for me. God promised to be there, and He was. Here's our story:

God's Promises Give Us Hope and Peace

<u>Marty's perspective</u>:

God's faithfulness to us has been clear through all our years together and especially as our family dealt with Vern's cancer diagnosis. Vern faced the physical impact of illness and treatment. But for me the challenges were layered: emotional, spiritual, and physical in a different way. Hearing or reading the "C" word in relation to a loved one is staggering and scary. Denial is a normal response, and I certainly had moments of disbelief. Vern was rarely sick, and in fact had not been in a hospital since his birth! His was the first cancer diagnosis in his family. Unbelievable.

Vern's illness unfolded during the winter of 2013. A beloved parishioner had died unexpectedly, and Vern, as her pastor, tended to the details of her funeral, burial, and cared for her husband. This occurred during a bitterly cold spell. Vern didn't feel well, unusual for him. He couldn't get warm, very unusual for the guy who was always hot. I'd come home from work, and he'd be bundled under blankets with a space heater aimed his direction. After a bit of encouragement, Vern scheduled a doctor visit, also unusual. Over the next few months, tests and more tests were administered. "Lymphoma": That's what the doctor expected a biopsy would reveal.

Vern's biopsy was scheduled for the day after Easter, Easter Monday, 2014. But Easter Sunday, Vern was in the pulpit. And all four of our kids were with me in the pew. Our baby, Kristen, was 13 and in 8th grade. Travis was 23, Heidi was 26, and Erik, 28. Our older two had not planned to be home for Easter, but they and their significant others (now their spouses), Shaun and Jayni, changed plans to support Vern and me as we prepared for the final diagnostic test.

Isaiah 43:2 assures us that when we pass through the waters, God is with us. God's presence was clear as our family joined together to support Vern, bolstered by our faithful church family. Our youngest child Kristen sang Laura Story's "Blessings" during the Easter service. I blinked back tears hearing the message of the song and it was our 13-year-old daughter who was giving me courage and inspiration through her song.

It reminded me of James 1:12:

> "Blessed is the man who remains steadfast under trial, for when he has stood the test he will receive the crown of life, _which God has promised to those who love him_ (ESV)."
> ~ The Holy Bible, English Standard Version. ESV® Text Edition: 2016. Copyright ©2001 by Crossway Bibles

There it was, so plain and simple. God promised the crown of life to Vern, to me, to our family, and church family. What more did we need? And what did we need to receive this crown? LOVE! It might seem like the apostle is urging obedience, but what he says is "Blessed," or "Exceedingly happy" is he who remains steadfast under trial. You can actually be filled with joy during a trial because God has made a promise to those who recognize the free gift of God's grace and respond in love. The crown of life is not a reward for our obedience. The reception of the crown of life is the result of faith-producing love which causes helpless sinners to cling to Christ, the Savior of the world. The Gospel promises us an inheritance which only Christ has earned.

The **truth** here is that the crown we wear belongs to Jesus Christ, our Savior and Victor through _every_ trial. He will carry us through every dark place to victory. We cling to Him in love and He promises "never to leave us or forsake us." Our 13-year-old daughter, who knew her dad would have his biopsy the next morning gave me joy, courage, and inspiration to face one of the darkest trials of my life.

Pastor Vernon Lintvedt, Blessed Savior Lutheran Church, and
Marty Lintvedt, Licensed Professional Counselor

> The crown of life is not a reward for our obedience.
> The reception of the crown of life is the result of faith-
> producing love which causes helpless sinners to cling to
> Christ, the Savior of the world.
> The Gospel promises us an inheritance
> which only Christ has earned.

2 Corinthians 12:9 … "My grace is sufficient for you, for my power is made perfect in weakness."

The doctor had tried to prepare us for the diagnosis. But I still hoped the test would be negative. It was not. We learned the things important for families dealing with a cancer diagnosis, including treatment protocol, possible side effects of medications and treatments, navigating insurance, and on and on.

Our family, church family, and friends showed the face of Christ in so many ways. God's grace was sufficient, his presence was sure. Some who'd fought his or her own cancer battle shared helpful tips for dealing with chemo, chills, diet, even clothing. Others dropped by with a meal now and then. One faithful friend regularly called Vern and stayed on the phone when Vern would nod off, exhausted by his disease and treatment. My daughter's friends baked cookies and cupcakes for us. Others helped with transportation when I couldn't get back from my office, which was 35 miles from our home, or from the hospital in time to pick Kristen up from her evening high school theater production rehearsals.

While Vern experienced the physical impact of cancer treatment, he remained steady emotionally. As I handled roles we typically shared on my own and navigated this new normal, I was at times exhausted, often anxious, frequently fearful of the possible outcomes. Vern's steadiness reflected his unwavering faith in the God who would not and did not leave. I kept silent about my fears and God provided his strength to face the unknown.

Vern completed his chemotherapy. Things were looking good. Vern was in remission. Our daughter, Heidi, married Shaun in Fall, 2014 and her dad officiated. It was a joyous time! Then in 2015, the cancer returned. This time the doctors recommended an autologous stem cell transplant, which is a stem cell transplant that uses stem cells from one's own body. This is a difficult, brutal process. Preparation includes several rounds of chemo and culminates with a long hospital stay during which the patient undergoes the transplant, and a long recovery. It was frightening to think of the risks involved, but the hope for a cure was very encouraging.

> Isaiah 41:10: "… fear not, for I am with you; be not dismayed for I am your God; I will strengthen you, I will help you, I will uphold you with my righteous hand."

Pastor Vernon Lintvedt, Blessed Savior Lutheran Church, and
Marty Lintvedt, Licensed Professional Counselor

Cancer is scary. Cancer is expensive, even with insurance. God is faithful. As I mentioned earlier, the face of Christ shown through many who came alongside us during this time. One of our church members planned a fundraiser to help offset the costs of Vern's treatment. This was no ordinary bake sale. Our parishioner and friend, Ed, built a Human Foosball Court and promoted a tournament in the local media. Yes, there was a concession stand, selling hot dogs, sodas, and baked goods. And then there was the tournament, which was a huge success! Church members, neighbors, community members, school friends, and teachers turned out to participate and support Vern. We were and are so grateful for the generosity of so many saints.

On May 20, 2015 Vern was admitted to Siteman Cancer Center in St. Louis. That day I wrote in a Facebook post:

> "This is the day which the LORD has made; Let us rejoice and be glad in it." Psalm 118:24 (NASB 1995)
> New American Standard Bible®, Copyright © 1960, 1971, 1977, 1995 by The Lockman Foundation. All rights reserved.

> "Today Vern heads to Siteman Cancer Center. After more chemo he will undergo a stem cell transplant. Vern's very own stem cells have been harvested already. It seems as if we are watching God's mighty hand at work, amazing medical advances unfolding before our eyes.

"Thank you to each friend and family member lifting Vern and our family in prayer, and for accompanying us on this journey. Rejoicing in this day!"

The following was written by my daughter Heidi to her dad, and I included it in my message. Vern had played linebacker on his high school football team:

"Linebackers are the portrait of toughness and grit that epitomizes the game of football. To be a linebacker, you must be strong, a leader, physically and mentally tough, not afraid to put your head in there and make a collision.

"Check the stats, and you'll see that the linebackers almost always lead the team in the number of tackles. Dad, here is one more thing to tackle for that linebacker still inside you. Kick some lymphoma butt today! I love you!"

Moses gave us a powerful message to comfort us during our wilderness journey:

Be strong and courageous. Do not fear or be in dread of them, for it is the LORD your God who goes with you. He will not leave you or forsake you." (Deuteronomy 31:6, ESV)

Bottom line for me is that <u>God promised He would never leave us</u>. <u>His presence was sure throughout Vern's cancer journey</u>. It was communicated through friends, family, colleagues, doctors, and nurses. And <u>God promised to strengthen us for our trials</u>.

As Isaiah writes:

But they who wait for the Lord shall renew their strength;
they shall mount up with wings like eagles;
they shall run and not be weary;
they shall walk and not faint.
(Isaiah 40:30-31, ESV)

<u>And He did what He promised</u>! That was the only way we could have gotten to the other side of this. For Vern, his cancer battle was physically grueling. He put his head in, remained strong, confident in God's promises. Vern had a *hope* for recovery. But he was *sure* of God's presence.

For me, the cancer journey was an emotional roller coaster. I often felt I was on autopilot, frequently off balance. I needed to stay focused on the tasks at hand in order to keep my feet under me. But God, through his Word and through those he sent to walk with us time and again steadied me, kept me grounded.

> God promised He would never leave us.
> His presence was sure throughout Vern's cancer journey
> … God promised to strengthen us for our trials.

As of this writing, 2021, six years have passed since Vern's stem-cell treatment. Today he is cancer free, praise be to God! Vern trusted God at each step of his cancer journey, and he was unafraid. I confess at times I was scared. Vern's confidence in God *no matter the outcome* was an affirmation of God's promise of salvation to those who believe in Christ — the most precious promise of all.

> Vern's confidence in God *no matter the outcome* was an affirmation of God's promise of salvation to those who believe in Christ — the most precious promise of all.

Vern's Addendum:

Twenty-five years before I received my diagnosis of non-Hodgkin's lymphoma, I ministered to a young, 30-year-old Physical Ed teacher from my congregation who had the same diagnosis. All I could tell you *then* was that it was some form of cancer. I remember driving 150 miles or so to see Carol at the hospital in St Louis. The two-and-a-half-hour trip gave me time to pray and prepare my words for this short visit. I remember being totally aware that the expression on my face was probably communicating more strongly than my words. She was understandably fearful. I tried to the best of my ability to comfort her but my words seemed so ethereal to give her any comfort for this very real and dreaded disease, not to mention the treatment that was distorting her previously healthy appearance.

I've seen that "look" on the faces of those who saw *me* during my treatment. Of course, when the chemo starts to take effect, the hair starts falling out. The beard also disappeared. I barely recognized myself! During my treatment I did a wedding for a couple in my church. When the couple posted a few pictures on Facebook, someone I didn't know commented about the weird looking guy in the photo. It was a picture of the couple and me. The couple could have been on the cover of any high fashioned glamour magazine, and since we were the only ones in the frame, I couldn't dismiss the comment by pointing to someone else.

One honest young man whom I confirmed when he was in junior high school, who didn't always filter his words said, "Pastor Vern looks like Uncle Fester from the Addams Family." I laughed and thanked him for being so honest. So many others would try to make me feel better by saying things like, "You look good." Or, "You look ten years younger without your beard." I have a pretty good sense of humor so Uncle Fester being a Hollywood celebrity was a compliment.

It's one thing to see your youthful appearance transform and quite another to know that cancer in any form can be a death sentence.

Thankfully, my doctors were all very hopeful of my condition. They even used the word "curable." I had never heard the words "cancer" and "curable" in the same sentence. It's amazing what cancer research has accomplished in twenty-five years. But my story is one of those where everything just "fell into place" for me. We called that perfect plan not coincidence but a "God-incidence."

I didn't have any knowledge of where to go, or which doctor to see. But the Lord had this whole plan already worked out. Every step I took in this foreign medical field just seemed to work out perfectly. From the day I got the results of the biopsy to the end of my treatment, I have had perfect peace. Even through the hard days of chemo treatments and having to go another round after thinking we got it the first round, I just thought, "Okay, what's next?" Where did that peace come from? There's a passage of scripture answers that question best for me.

> "Rejoice in the Lord always; again I will say, rejoice. Let your reasonableness be known to everyone. The *Lord is at hand*; do not be anxious about anything, but in everything by prayer and supplication with thanksgiving let your requests be made known to God. And *the peace of God*, which surpasses all understanding, will guard your hearts and your minds in Christ Jesus." (Philippians 4:4-7, ESV)

There is a lot to unpack in these four verses but there are two very special promises in this passage I grasped onto throughout my entire life and especially during my bout with cancer.

The first promise was this: **The Lord is at hand**.

I do not remember a time in my life that I did not believe the Lord was at my side. To be honest, there were times I had hoped He wasn't there because of the things I was doing which I knew to be outside His will for me. My faith (a total gift from above) taught me that He was always there, guiding and directing even when I was unmindful of His presence! Every time I came to my senses, that promise renewed my joy!

Saint Paul said it this way:

> "The saying is trustworthy, for:
> If we have died with him, we will also live with him;
> if we endure, we will also reign with him;
> if we deny him, he also will deny us;
> if we are faithless, he remains faithful —
> for he cannot deny himself.
> (2 Timothy 2:11–13, ESV)

Oh yes, you can be unfaithful to God without denying Him! I never denied God, but I certainly found myself being "unfaithful" to Him. On the other hand, God cannot not betray who He is. He cannot go outside His nature or His amazing character and renege on His promises. And with the Lord's promise to be "at hand," came God's perfect peace. This truth spoke calm to my soul and my spirit was reassured every time I heard or read the words of Scripture: "I will never leave you nor forsake you!" (Hebrews 13:5, ESV)

God cannot not betray who He is.
He cannot go outside His nature or His amazing character and renege on His promises.

King David had this unshakable confidence in God's saving presence. He said,

"He who dwells in the shelter of the Most High
will abide in the shadow of the Almighty.
I will say to the LORD, "My refuge and my
fortress, my God, in whom I trust.
For he will deliver you from the snare of the
fowler and from the deadly pestilence."
(Psalm 91:1–2, ESV)

Because the Lord is at hand, He is also "my refuge and my fortress." There is no evil that Almighty God cannot overcome. Jesus proved that on the Day of His Resurrection! And because the Lord is at hand, we need not fear anything! Not even death!

The second promise I clung to was this: **The Peace of God**.

If you have ever had an MRI or PET or other medical scans you know how nerve-racking they can be, especially for the claustrophobic (which I am not!). They put you in the narrow tube of this imposing machine that looks and sounds like it might just teleport you to another Star Trek galaxy. Then the technician says, "Now don't move." About one minute into the fifteen to twenty-minute procedure you can feel a strong twitching urge in your limbs. The way I would overcome the loud metallic noise and the twitching was to say the Lord's Prayer or the 23rd Psalm over and over again. It worked every time! As I confirmed the Lord as my Shepherd, a peace came over me like a soothing bath.

As I look back, the Peace of God came to me in two special ways which I've have come to really appreciate even to this day. The important part is understanding God's peace is wholly a gift! And that gift of peace comes in person. Here's how Jesus communicated His peace to me. It comes from the pen of the beloved Apostle John:

> "These things I have spoken to you while I am still with you. But the Helper, the Holy Spirit, whom the Father will send in my name, he will teach you all things and bring to your remembrance all that I have said to you. <u>Peace I leave with you; my peace I give to you</u>. Not as the world gives do I give to you. Let not your

hearts be troubled, neither let them be afraid."
(John 14:25-27, ESV)

The Holy Spirit is a mystery to us, yet <u>Jesus promised His</u> <u>coming and indwelling power and peace</u>. Jesus explained the mystery to Nicodemus saying,

> "The wind blows where it wishes, and you hear its sound, but you do not know where it comes from or where it goes. So it is with everyone who is born of the Spirit." (John 3:8, ESV)

The mystery is heightened by the Apostle Paul who describes the indwelling Spirit in us as the same Spirit who raised Jesus from the dead:

> "If the Spirit of him who raised Jesus from the dead dwells in you, he who raised Christ Jesus from the dead will also give life to your mortal bodies through his Spirit who dwells in you." (Romans 8:11, ESV)

We cannot see the wind but we can feel it. We can see its effect, just like we see the effect when a hurricane blows through. Because the Spirit of God is not perceptible to our eyes, we tend to question His existence. But God knows our weakness and our spiritual blindness, so He opens our eyes by showing us the effect of the Spirit. God has not only given us the place where He locates His Spirit's presence invisibly, but He reveals His Spirit in a very concrete way, and that is through the Church. Oh, what a blessing the Church of Christ, where God manifests and delivers His peace.

As a pastor with over 30 years of ministering to people with life-threatening issues, I have witnessed and been inspired by the peace of God at work of His people in the church. My flock will know some of the names below who have received such peace as they courageously faced death.

> **Marie** was a young and spry 60-year-old wife, mother and grandmother when she received the diagnosis of cancer. I remember her palpable anxiety and fear when she came into my office to give me the news. Her fear factor was at 8 or 9 on a scale of 10. A year or so after heavy chemo treatments, when the doctor said, "We've done everything we can …" her fear literally came to an abrupt halt. From 8 or 9 to 0!

> In the week of her death, I was blessed to witness this saint comforting her tearful 90-year-old father, and encouraging her sobbing adolescent grand-kids to honor their parents and above all, to trust in the Lord.

> **Ed and Diana** were married after both their first spouses had passed away from cancer. Imagine what it must have been like for them to trust in

God's promise of peace while raising their very young blended family in the throes of their own personal grief. Far from abandoning God, they continued to share their faith: Ed, by serving as an elder and caring for our church property, and Diana, by her unique gift of writing a dozen or more published Christian Romance novels.

Keith is like a brother to me because we have been through so much together. Keith lost his first and second wife to cancer, but continues to show his faith by his active participation in worship to God and in service to others. He is regarded by members of his own family and surprisingly by the families of his deceased wives, as the patriarch.

One of the most beautiful pictures I have of him was taken at the funeral home where we celebrated the life of his second wife. In a meditative moment, after the crowd dispersed except for family, Keith is sitting on a large couch in front of the casket with his adult kids and step-kids behind him, and eight grandkids seated beside and covering him like a weighted comfort blanket. It was moving to say the least.

Gwen is an octogenarian who is currently enduring an inoperable and incurable brain tumor. If you are picturing her in your mind's eye as a little old woman lying in bed, curled up in a fetal position and covered in blankets all day long, you've got the wrong picture. If she and her husband Wayne (who is also valiantly battling cancer) aren't visiting relatives, they are in church every Sunday, smiling and praising God openly with everyone they greet, thanking God for every day and every breath. Both Gwen and Wayne (a retired Coast Guard officer) have this unyielding, loyal and devoted faith in Christ as their Savior and daily grasp hold of His promise of their resurrected life to come!

Dave and Loriann, Don and Laura, Eric and Mary, Perry and Diane, Jim and Christi, Joan, Bret and April, and Carl are living saints who are still grieving the loss of children. Then there are those who are still secretly carrying the sorrow for the children they lost in the womb or at birth.

I marvel at the faith of these beloved people of God who are standing firm in the promises of God, in spite of their heartbreaking losses. I ask myself, how is it possible not to be angry with God in those circumstances? How is it possible to worship God who, from our perspective, can seem to heal or to take a life arbitrarily? What sustains these believers in their grief? It is undoubtedly the manifold promises of God which the Holy Spirit whispers into their hearts like a gentle breeze, softly speaking peace to their souls!

> What sustains these believers in their grief? It is undoubtedly the manifold promises of God which the Holy Spirit whispers into their hearts like a gentle breeze, softly speaking peace to their souls!

Marty

Probably the most underappreciated person in my life who has had to endure my weird sense of humor, my moodiness, and my stubbornness, all which have come out more prominently during my treatment and recovery, was my wife Marty. She was born and raised in the Lutheran faith. The heart of that faith is the grace and mercy of God toward sinners. All human efforts are the *outcome* of divine favor freely given, and not the reason for that favor. This teaching led Marty to live graciously and generously. No doubt the words, "Grace, mercy and peace be to you from God our heavenly Father and our Lord and Savior, Jesus, the Christ" (the words I use to begin each sermon), have stuck in her. She is one of the most perfect examples I know of someone who displays and utilizes the peace of God in her personal life and career. How she got there is a miracle to me.

Marty grew up quickly as a youth. Those gifts of God were forged like steel in the fires of life. Her mother was diagnosed with schizophrenia when she was a young adolescent. Her father was an alcoholic. While you wouldn't wish these circumstances upon any young child, in spite of their issues, Marty's parents were devout Christians and amazingly communicated the love and faithfulness of God in Jesus. Prayers for the healing of those illnesses were sought, but not answered in the way most of us would have liked. It's in these kinds of life-trials one can experience the absolute emptiness of hope and a life devoid of peace. But those trials didn't crush the Spirit of God in Marty or her parents, in spite of their disabilities. The Spirit of God was graciously imparted and strengthened their faith as the promised peace carried them through every trial.

As a result of God's presence and peace, the Lord has given Marty the freedom to serve out of pure love. She almost always responds (no one is perfect) to situations and people from a heart of gratitude to God. Her love and support are sincere and real. As we were making our last revisions for this chapter, she mentioned to me that there were times that she didn't feel up to going to church during my treatment, but she felt that she needed to reassure our church that all was well. What she learned was that they were there for her, too, with tons of love and support. That's how the church works.

Did I know that she had those qualities when I married her? Yes, I was aware. But going through the harsh treatments of cancer, including the fatigue and weakness, made me even more aware just how powerful the gifts of faith, hope, and love were embedded in her soul! Her quiet witness was an inspiration to me and our church during the whole time of my treatment and recovery.

Marty and I are in wholehearted agreement that the Holy Spirit has definitely been at work, as evidenced by the effects of His invisible presence and His visible presence in the church. We recognize that we are the blessed beneficiaries of His peace.

I didn't know if healing from cancer was in God's plan for me, but His promises remain sure and reliable even if there is a change, like the return of cancer. Individually and as a couple, Marty and I have had to drop our best laid plans as unforeseen crises have interrupted our lives over our time together. We weren't always happy with the circumstances we found ourselves in, but over the years we have learned that God's plan was always best, even when we couldn't see it at the time.

> … His promises remain sure and reliable
> even if there is a change …

The miraculous resurrection story of Jesus is something that was spiritually implanted deep inside us from our childhood days. We know that God has given us more grace than we deserve. This wasn't learned over night, but now we are quicker to recognize that <u>our plans are always subject to change for the greater plan of God</u>. What keeps that flexibility to conform our plans to God's is <u>His awesome promise that "nothing shall separate us from the love of God in Christ Jesus,"</u> absolutely *nothing*! Nothing can separate us from His presence nor the peace He brings.

> ... <u>our plans are always subject to change for the greater plan of God</u>. What keeps that flexibility to conform our plans to God's is <u>His awesome promise that "nothing shall separate us from the love of God in Christ Jesus,"</u> absolutely *nothing*! Nothing can separate us from His presence nor the peace He brings.

Death is the necessary ending to the final chapter of our earthly life, and God Himself determines that day and hour. But everyone who puts their trust in the Lord has a pre-written final chapter beyond death. Our life's story involves a personal resurrection and a new beginning of life eternal.

And because of God's promises and His resurrection power, the beautiful words of the prophet Jeremiah have as much meaning for us now as they did to the Israelites of old. Israel had been razed to the ground and her people were taken into captivity by the Babylonians. Talk about your plans going awry! Having witnessed what looked like the total obliteration of the Holy City, and his nation in exile, Jeremiah, under the inspiration of the Holy Spirit, wrote a letter to their grieving hearts which includes this glorious promise:

> "For I know the plans I have for you," declares the LORD, "plans to prosper you and not to harm you, plans to give you hope and a future." (Jeremiah 29:11)

Got plans? That's great! Entrust them to the Lord. But should those plans be disrupted, take comfort: the Spirit of God is at work for something far greater!

> "Eye has not seen, nor ear heard, Nor have entered into the heart of man the things which God has prepared for those who love Him." (1 Corinthians 2:9, NKJV)

It's not all a complete mystery. We've actually been told quite a bit. Here's the promise/sneak preview of God's gracious plan for all of us:

> "… we await a Savior, the Lord Jesus Christ, <u>who will transform our lowly body to be like his glorious body,</u> by the power that enables him even to subject all things to himself." (Philippians 3:20–21, ESV)

Please let me add a personal note to end this chapter. Marty and I have been married for 40 years as of this writing.

Pastor Vernon Lintvedt, Blessed Savior Lutheran Church, and
Marty Lintvedt, Licensed Professional Counselor

We have experienced the ups and downs of life, great joys, and great disappointments. We have argued and reconciled so many times it would be hard to count.

We are real people with real problems but above all, we are a couple who have experienced mercy and grace from a real God in a real way. God, who accepted us as we were in spite of our messed-up lives, honored us by His presence and real promises for an extraordinary future. It is His presence in us, and the precious promises we have experienced, that cause us to pray that our story gives you hope.

This prayer is for everyone who needs some assurance as the end of the ages draws near:

> "May the God of hope fill you with all joy and peace as you trust in him, so that you may overflow with hope by the power of the Holy Spirit."
> (Romans 15:13, ESV)

*****

From Vernon:

Over 50 years ago I met Glen Aubrey in our high school choir. In 1970, Glen was leading a Gospel Quartet and "The Revelaires" were looking for a baritone and invited me to join. Not really knowing what I was getting into, I jumped in.

Every morning before dawn, for about two to three weeks, I met Glen at his parents' home (Bud and Zela), and rehearsed until I had the repertoire memorized.

Glen's mother would fix breakfast and read a passage of scripture while we scarfed down some eggs, bacon, and some toast! Then we ran to school to get to our Chamber Choir rehearsals at 7 a.m. That was the beginning of our lifelong relationship. During a rough couple of years back in 2013-2015, while I was dealing with Non-Hodgkin's Lymphoma, Glen would call and check up on me at least once a week.

Glen is not only a production "machine," but a compassionate and caring friend. Only God knows how much my faith in God grew as a result of this treasured friendship.

~ Vernon Lintvedt, October, 2021

From Glen:

Vernon Lintvedt is the Pastor of Blessed Savior Lutheran Church in O'Fallon, Illinois. He and Marty, his wife, who is a Licensed Professional Counselor, have been serving in ministries for 27 years as of 2021. Vern is a great friend from high school. He is an example of God fulfilling His promises to care for His children through Vern's ministry to his flock,

*Pastor Vernon Lintvedt, Blessed Savior Lutheran Church, and
Marty Lintvedt, Licensed Professional Counselor*

along with the full support of Marty, and his health victory over cancer.

I have treasured Vernon's close friendship for 50+ years. His ministry and testimony still encourage and inspire me! I am so grateful to God for Vernon, our association, and ministry endeavors down through the years!

~ Glen Aubrey, October, 2021

*****

My Child, Did You Know?

Rick Redd, MD
Author: *All-In Or Nothing * Master Your Destiny* and
All-In Or Nothing Beyond Retirement
Published by Creative Team Publishing
www.creativeteampublishing.com
© 2020 and 2021, respectively
Order Rick's books at www.all-inornothing.com

"Wealth" is a word with multiple connotations. Some might say it is a six-figure bank account. Others believe it is a balanced, diversified investment portfolio. filled with high-value properties, stocks, precious metals, and bonds. Still others put great value in a large family, being a successful writer, musician, or CEO, having a steady, worthwhile job, being in good health, or having a peaceful existence.

How you define wealth depends on where you put your priorities. If your focus is on things physical, emotional, or intellectual, what you believe and conclude may naturally follow along these lines of thought.

But how do you define wealth spiritually? As one who has not yet met God personally, and has never been reconciled to Him, spiritual wealth may have no meaning. But, as a believer in the triune God, does your definition of wealth change? If so, how? More to the point, as a Christian, how do you know if you are wealthy?

Consider 2 Peter 1:1-4 in the New King James Version of the Bible (NKJV) (Author emphasis in italics added):

> 1 Simon Peter, a bondservant and apostle of Jesus Christ,
>
> To those who have obtained like precious faith with us by the righteousness of our God and Savior Jesus Christ:
>
> 2 Grace and peace be multiplied to you in the knowledge of God and of Jesus our Lord, 3 as His divine power has given to us all things that pertain to life and godliness, through the knowledge of Him who called us by glory and virtue, 4 by which have been given to us *exceedingly great and precious promises,* that through these you may be partakers of the divine nature, having escaped the corruption that is in the world through lust.

A number of points from this passage become immediately apparent to me:

1) The passage was written by the Apostle Simon Peter to Christians in Rome, but also to those throughout the world, that is, those who professed a belief in, and a dependence upon Jesus Christ as Savior and Lord (Verse 1b).
2) God, through His divine power, has given the members of His family His exceedingly great and precious promises (Verse 4a).
3) These promises form the foundation for spiritual wealth.
4) As we become aware of these promises and apply them in our lives, we develop a more Christ-like attitude and behavior (divine nature) and we will avoid the obstacles (corruption) in the world which might lead us to fall away from the faith (4b).

All the promises of God, as outlined throughout the Bible, are specifically given to those of us who have accepted Jesus Christ as Savior and Lord, who are now endeavoring to live the life of faith from that point forward — with one exception.

The promise of salvation is for **everyone**, especially non-believers. John 3:16-17 says "16 For God so loved the world that He gave His only begotten Son, that whoever believes in Him should not perish but have everlasting life. 17 For God did not send His Son into the world to condemn the world, but that the world through Him might be saved." (NKJV)

Romans 10:9-10 expounds "9 ...if you confess with your mouth the Lord Jesus and believe in your heart that God has raised Him from the dead, you will be saved. 10 For with the heart one believes unto righteousness, and with the mouth confession is made unto salvation." (NKJV)

All of the other promises of God in the Bible are addressed to the members of His family, His children only. Unless you are a citizen of heaven, you will gain no benefit from these promises. You can claim them all day long, but unless you know Him as Savior and Lord, you will gain no power. There is no such thing as an illegal immigrant in heaven.

God's promises are *valid* because they originate from God; He is Truth and He is faithful. Moreover, He has the ability to *fulfill* these promises because He is omniscient, omnipresent, and omnipotent. *Only* God can give them. In verse 4 of 2 Peter 1, the verb *given* is in the passive form, which means that they were given in times past and continue to be given now. As Believers, we inherit these promises at the moment of salvation.

God's promises are of immeasurable *value*. Because they originate from God Himself, they cannot be anything less than perfect. He makes no junk, nothing substandard.

Everything that emanates from Him is excellent, superb, and magnificent.

God's promises, as we will see, make us amazingly wealthy, but they are of value to us as individuals *only* if we are aware of them (knowledge) and when we apply (*appropriate*/accept/use/claim) them in our lives. In the same way that money, a source of material wealth, is of no benefit unless it is used (spent), this is no less true of spiritual wealth.

The divine nature that we develop as we mature in Christ (referred to in verse 4b of 1 Peter 1) may be more completely defined as loving God, respecting Him, and doing His will, while glorifying Him in all that we do. This becomes manifest personally as we grow more toward righteousness, identifying and meeting the needs of others, and leaving a notable, positive legacy from which others grow and benefit.

There are countless promises from God in the scriptures. Some are unconditional; they apply to us no matter what we do. Others are conditional upon things we need to do in order to receive the promise. Most the promises apply throughout history; a few (such as the promise of bearing children in old age, or the promise of a lamb to prevent sacrificing a son), refer to specific times or specific individuals. These specific promises still give us insight into the nature and character of the God we serve.

Let's examine a few of the promises, and see how they may apply:

1. Romans 5:6-11 stipulates that we are reconciled to God through the death of Christ. We are *guaranteed* this heritage of God (our Father), Christ Jesus (His Son and our Savior), and the Holy Spirit when we believe that Christ is Lord of our lives.

2. John 10: 27-30 stipulates that we have eternal salvation, a permanent home in heaven (John 14:1-3) after we finish our course on earth.

3. 1 John 1:9 guarantees that because God is faithful, our sins will be forgiven *every day* if we confess them.

4. Hebrews 13:5 promises that He will *never* leave us or forsake us, *no matter what*. John 14:16 holds that The Holy Spirit will *always* be with us to comfort us or assist us. What an empowering thought!

5. God promises to strengthen us in Isaiah 41: 9-10 and in Psalm 46:1-3.

6. He guarantees to meet our *daily* needs in Matthew 6:25, 31-32 and bear our burdens *daily* in Psalm 68:19.

7. 2 Corinthians 1:3, 4 stipulates that He will comfort us in *all* our afflictions when we are troubled.

8. 1 Corinthians 10:13 says that He will put limits on any trials we encounter, and provide a way of escape.

9. James 1:5 guarantees that when we ask for wisdom (God's perspective), God will grant it liberally and without demeaning us.

Only God can fulfill these promises. No one else on earth (no parent, relative, spouse, or friend), no matter how well-meaning or selfless, can do these things for you. *Only* God can suffice. What a treasure trove of value we have! What a gift from God who loves us!

I have been a Christian for many years, but I was either never taught about appropriating the promises of God or I failed to realize the importance and the relevance (practicality) of these promises when they were explained to me. Thankfully, I have grown in knowledge and faith over the years, but not nearly as quickly as I would have, had I studied the promises more. They would have guided me in my efforts to be more Christ-like in my daily walk. They would have also served as a "danger" sign for obstacles and potholes in the road ahead.

Here are some other examples of the wealth we hold now, as Believers:

10. Matthew 11:28-30 promises us rest for our body and our mind, and peace that surpasses all understanding is guaranteed in Philippians 4:4-7.
11. Psalm 32:8 guarantees that God will give you direction for your life. Moreover, He will counsel you while He has His eye on you. That is personalized service
12. God will give us the desires of our heart when we delight in Him (Psalm 37:4).

13. Psalm 92:12 stipulates that we will be strong and fruitful, with abounding energy, as we age. That is especially comforting to me! In fact, I just finished writing a book, ***All-In Or Nothing <u>Beyond</u> Retirement*** (please see www.all-inornothing.com), about options we have available to us to arrest or forestall the effects of aging. All of these options branch from this promise.

14. Moreover, in Isaiah 40:31 the Lord promises to renew the strength of those who hope in Him. To soar on wings like an eagle, run and not grow weary, and walk without being faint appeals to me greatly.

15. Psalm 103:1-3 promises that God will heal us in times of sickness. Doctors may help, but God brings about the healing of body and mind. After spending many years in the service of medicine, I can strongly attest to that fact.

There are no accidents in this life for those who know and love the Lord. He guides and directs our every step. There are no exceptions! We may initially believe God allows "bad" events to happen *to* us; how refreshing, though, when we are persuaded that God has allowed those very events to happen *for* our benefit, our growth, or our outreach to others. How could He do less; it is not in His character to give us anything but the best.

I came to this realization in 1991 when I had a motor-vehicle accident. Thankfully, I was not seriously hurt, but I learned through that experience that there are times when I have no control over what is happening, and I must "let go, and ask God" to intervene. He faithfully will. As I have recounted that event to others, I am constantly reminded of His power and His willingness to intercede on behalf of His children.

Many times, I have asked myself how my life might have changed *if ...*

1) I would have grown up at a different time in history or in a different place
2) I would have had different parents
3) I had not applied myself diligently in school and continued to learn after I left school
4) I would have gone to Stanford instead of the United States Military Academy at West Point
5) I would have served in an artillery unit in the United States Army instead of going to medical school
6) I would have become a cardiologist instead of a radiologist
7) I would have gone to Augsburg, Germany in 1981, and worked for and with a man who eventually became the Surgeon General (3 stars) of the Army; could he have helped me to become a general officer too?
8) I had never met my wife, Julie

At every fork in the road, the Lord nudged me in the way I should go. While it may be fun to speculate, "What might have been" serves no useful purpose. While the results of my life may not have been the same, I am convinced that I received the best I could ask for. The God of the universe was at my side, and I was doing His will as best I knew it.

Now that I am no longer working a "job," I have the luxury of time and experience to look back and reevaluate the parts of my life that came before. I am blessed to live in the best country on earth, despite all of its current problems and challenges. I can still choose how I will spend the last years of my life, with God's guidance. I assure you that I am doing everything I can physically, emotionally, intellectually, and spiritually to "finish strong," not only for myself, but also for others whom I care about and for my country.

The Lord is my constant companion; he is still mentoring my every step. I know not what lies ahead, but I do know that He has promised to be there with me no matter the circumstances.

One last promise came to mind as I was finishing my thoughts:

2 Chronicles 7:14 stipulates,

> "If my people which are called by my name, shall humble themselves, and pray and seek My face, and turn from their wicked ways, then will I (God) hear from heaven, and will forgive their sin, and will heal their land." (NKJV)

With all of the disruption and tumult that we are currently experiencing in the United States of America, the promise of 2 Chronicles 7:14 still holds true. Notice, though, that this promise is conditional. He will restore our land and our place of leadership in the world *if and only if* we seek Him and honor Him by placing Him in His rightful position as Leader and Sovereign and Lord of this nation. How this will happen is anyone's guess, but based on the depths to which we may have fallen, I suspect it will be miraculous! There will be no doubt in anyone's mind that God's mighty Hand was evident.

Let's all pray to that end. And in the meantime, let's continue to live expectantly and faithfully, honoring Him in all that we do.

Glory be to God! I'll see you on life's road … there is much work left to be done.

May God continue to bless you greatly!

*****

References:

o Sermons on cassette tape (2 Peter 1) from Pastor Tom Rodgers and Pastor Reggie Coe. Grace Church, Wichita Falls, TX.
o Stanley, Charles F. *God's Precious Promises* http://www.bing.com/videos/search?q=Claiming+

God%27s+principles+charles+stanley+you+tube+video

- o Swindoll, Charles R. *Swindoll's New Testament Insights (James, 1 & 2 Peter)*. Grand Rapids, MI: Zondervan, 2010.

*****

From Rick:

Glen and I have never met in person, believe it or not. I got his name from a valued friend of mine, as an excellent Christian publisher. I was thinking about writing a book relating to holistic health, and asked for his opinion. After countless hours on the phone, four books and two chapters in Glen's new works (**God's Plan Unfolding** and **God's Promises**) during the past two years, Glen and I have become great friends.

Glen is a consummate professional; I plugged into his system quickly and we were soon exchanging information at a rapid rate. His input was invaluable. Sometimes he suggested more information, or a more accurate word, or elimination of a pesky grammatical error (dangling participles seem to be my specialty). He always seemed to work with my "system" as well (including my research, outlining, rough draft, overread, and text/graphic art submission), so the "order of march" was organized and specific on both ends. He spurred my projects forward, all the while, helping me remain motivated and productive. I never felt that he was being critical of my work. Enthusiasm abounded!

Glen is committed to the excellence of producing Christian-based books of the highest quality. He "walks the talk" of a Christ led life. His team brings expertise and excellence to the process, which gives a novice writer like me a great deal of confidence. Many thanks, Glen. It was an honor to be asked to contribute to this anthology of magnificent work, **God's Promises**.

~ Rick Redd, MD, December 2021

From Glen:

My life has been dramatically and positively affected by my association with Dr. Rick Redd. He is a holistic, retired radiologist with a decided accent on health: physically, mentally, emotionally, and spiritually. His writing is clear and well researched. His resources are many and I have willingly availed myself of them often, and with earnest desire.

I have quoted him often to family and friends; indeed, there are many in my personal and business networks who have benefitted from his expertise, compassion, knowledge, and wisdom.

I have told Rick many times over two years that his instructions regarding diet, vitamins, exercise, and more have "added years to my life" and "life to my years." It's true. I have adopted his often-stated phrase: "There are no accidents." I am convinced of this truth with every fiber of my being. Contemplating, then implementing major alterations in my own lifestyle, I witness positive differences nearly every day.

Rick's belief in the sovereignty of God inspires and provides impetus to those under his influence to endeavor to draw closer to God and His will for life and real living.

Rick is a Veteran and a staunch Patriot of the United States of America. He is conservative in at the core of who he is, and balanced in opinion and proclamation. I sincerely appreciate his "take" on current events and potential outcomes. He is one with whom I agree wholeheartedly.

What a pleasure to work with him on two major books and accompanying study guides. I warmly invite you to learn from him as I have, reading his works, taking in all he offers, and practically applying his truths and practices. Access this website for more information, and to order his literature: **www.all-inornothing.com**.

~ Glen Aubrey, December, 2021

*****

God Has No Downtime

Nancy Sidock
Poetess

I am no Bible scholar, as described by today's definition. I read and study the Word. It is with marked, conscious effort that I apply the great truths to my daily living.

The thoughts that God has no downtime came to mind after my complaining/prayer brought swift conviction. Earnestly, I had prayed for understanding. Why was He requiring me to be a vessel of servitude to strangers and friends in crisis? I had limited minutes of downtime as a caregiver for my husband, suffering with Stage 4 bone cancer. Surely, I qualified for uninterrupted porch sitting time. All I needed, (so I thought) and wanted for those downtime minutes, was to just sit on my porch and enjoy the smell and beauty of nature's abundant offering. Spring had finally decided to come out of hiding!

I cannot remember when I have not examined life, sought answers, and pressed the Lover of my Soul for more understanding. This statement is definitively more accurate now than it has ever been in my 73 years of having a dawning of light break the eastern sky.

One just does not have that many days and years of photons gathering, and not experience the hurt, disappointment, sickness, loss, defeat, rejection, and despair that has the covering we call "life."

I own various shapes and sizes of prisms hung in a window which catches the morning light. Depending on the weather or time of day, sometimes there will be no reflected color painting my wall. Ever so slightly I touch the nylon fishing string. The palomar knot has secured the diamond shaped prism for over 30 years. As the mother and grandmother to four Eagle Scouts, I did more than bake cookies. Searching, always searching for more light!

I remember well the cold winter day I stood close to the window, watching it snow, knowing the beauty of the moment would soon equate to an hour of shoveling. An unintentional heavy-hearted sigh created a quivering movement with the diamond shaped prism. Laughter, sweet refreshing laughter burst forth when color erupted across my wall. In that moment I felt a special closeness to my Friend.

Once I tried whistling to test the air movement. The conclusion that whistling is an art which I have not conquered, became very evident as I tried to recover from my coughing fit. Not one time in my life has anyone ever asked if I would like to learn to whistle. As I think about it, I have never seen a book written about whistling.

The wind, when downsized to an unseen movement of aerosols, especially on cold winter days, creeps in around the paned windows and moves the prisms simultaneously. In a glorious burst of highs and lows, colors swirl on the wall. Always felt, but never seen, that cold winter air serves a purpose as it conducts a silent symphony. The crescendo of color climbing higher up the wall and splashing across the ceiling is one of the very few benefits, I have decided, that comes from living in this older home built in 1931. History tells us that Congress adopted *The Star-Spangled Banner* as the national anthem on March 3rd of that year.

Constantly looking for the rainbow God promises after a storm, strengthens my weakness of impatience. It is a matter of timing. My time seems to be a little faster than the Lord's. His is always accurate. I most often seek the rainbow before the storm has passed through. The Lord alone controls the length of the storm.

The negatives and positives, stitched together with threads of God's grace and mercy make this covering called my life. Readily I accept I am blessed above measure! Many of the negatives, like a knotted thread have left deep wounds that were slow to heal. In the year 1995/96 I suffered with great mental anguish from the actions of another individual. This negative was my goodnight and good morning. Regardless of the times I desire to seclude myself, become passive with others, become impatient with God's timing, the Lord requires that I respond. Always I am given options!

Never more than two choices are offered up. Seek His light or suffer defeat.

No heavy-hearted sigh or flick of my finger will bring the rainbow when the thread knots. The Lord requires His blood-bought children to be the aerosols of a cool refreshing breeze to help others on their journey of life. Even when we desire downtime it is expected, from my point of view, to continue functioning in the fruits of the spirit. He never sleeps nor slumbers, and has no downtime.

My husband's diagnosis which momentarily produced panic, fear, and temporary breath-holding, has moved to the number one slot of life's negatives. What was life's normal has gradually become the abnormal. We made the decision to be positive. We had not embarked on a death watch; instead, we were looking for a victory flight to heaven.

Time, my time, my thoughts, my dreams, "my life" have become non-essential, except for the great importance of the expected and yes, the demanded energy required of a caregiver.

The truth is often stated that God promises to never leave or forsake us. I know this to be true. It's also true that God is using my hurts, impatience, and longings to stitch a greater testimony of my life.

Time is not my own. While I inhale/exhale second-by-second, seldom am I knowingly aware of the time reflected on a clock. When my stomach rumbles, I realize that while family was fed, I did not eat.

Purposely, in the stillness of the dark I now start my day very early. Sitting on the porch I find great pleasure in watching the orange and pinks streak the morning sky.

Caregiving is a self-consuming job. Mental relief that somehow transcends to physical refreshing, from the mundane tasks of being a caregiver, is abundantly provided when my mind is continually stayed on the Lover of my Soul. I have learned to press the Lord harder, and in my mind's eye I envision myself touching the hem of His garment.

When the porch sitting downtime is available, life is marked with moments of normalcy. Minutes have become an hour when I open my heart and mind in awareness to others also in need of a rainbow. When that place of submission is reached, the Lord, who has no downtime, and is the master chess player knows how to move those individuals into my life, and on my porch.

Her name is Carol. She lives across the street. A delightful lady whose face radiates love of life, always smiling even when life is not fair. If she sees me sitting on the porch, she makes her way across the street. We chat, we cry, and explore the mercies of God. Bonded by prayer. we like to think we have solved a few problems of the world. We have, in our little corner!

The light touches the prism of our soul and the beauty of color shines upon our day. It was Carol who provided the answer to a request for prayer in my seeking help. In my quest to make our home ready to sell, I needed physical help in downsizing our earthly possessions.

Her church hosted and sponsored missionary young men who give two years of their life to servitude. I struggled to comprehend why those young men would give of their time and not take payment. I wanted to compensate!

Carol, true to her word, connected me with young men who, over the course of several months, brought great joy to my life.

Immediately I recognized there was something different with the young men who gave several hours of their time weekly. Loading heavy boxes and furniture into my truck and unloading in storage or at local charities, was accomplished with patience. Never was there a time it became necessary to admonish them that they should be careful because of the contents.

The spirit of servitude to others and love for the Kingdom's work is the wind beneath their wings. Always smiling and kind, the young men brought light to my days.

We prayed together, and how refreshing it was to hear these young men pray the Word of God. To my delight, while they would not accept monetary compensation for their labor, they would allow me to feed them.

I introduced them to pizza from American Pie, a newly opened enterprise, whose owner was a chef from New York. Memories accumulated in my memory bank as we shared our life's adventures, our ups and downs, and introduced our families to each other by description and definition. My life has been made better because of Hammond, McCalister, Boston, and the others who were submitted to be a vessel of light.

Several times during my porch sitting time, especially early in the morning, I saw a lady walking. Her purposeful strides told me she was focused. She glanced toward me and said, "Good morning." I stopped contemplating my geraniums; I was compelled to acknowledge her. Her question, asking if she might come closer to see the flowers, received a swift, "Please do." Maria, the humble and sweet lady from Puerto Rico, has greatly blessed my life. Maria is also a caregiver. She has given her life to care for her mother, and her downtime is walking a mile each day. As I downsized, I gave "things" to Maria. Her care and concern for others was to help her and me in numerous ways.

It just so happens when you downsize, there is an abundance of items that are part of the reduction. I placed a plastic bin on the porch. We agreed that on the days the sign marked "Maria" was visible, there were items inside for her. This bin became a vessel that served both Maria and me. Purses, shoes, sheets, food, tools, and cooking vessels made their way into the bin. Maria would retrieve the items, then place the sign inside the bin and go on her way.

Occasionally my porch sitting time would mesh with her daily walk. On those days her burden of being a constant caregiver became a little lighter. We prayed on the porch for grace and mercy to be her portion. The light in her eyes would be brighter as she would turn to leave. A simple reasoning: someone acknowledged her life had purpose and she was making a difference. It was the day our timing aligned and as I was placing items in the bin that Maria rounded the corner. When she saw the box of box of laundry soap she began to cry. It was greatly needed. Over the course of the summer my time with Maria, although hit and miss, bonded us as friends. She became a prayer partner.

There came the day when my early morning porch sitting became different. The nipping coolness of the air made me shiver. The darkness of the night was lingering later and later. I noticed the potted geraniums had broken flowers and the soil had been disturbed. Squirrels who nested in the towering oak tree had decided to use my geraniums as a winter pantry. I knew the time had arrived to put my house on the market. The thought of another winter of shoveling snow was not in my future.

Where to go was a question that demanded an answer. Chuck did not want to take his victory flight from Maryland. The pull on my heart and the confirmation from the Lord became clear. His unseen hand was directing our lives. Within a week the home that I now referred to as "the house," was on the market. Three weeks later the "For Sale" sign was partially covered by the strip of wood reading "Sold." Final packing began. Friends made their way to our door to say good-bye. The only chairs not packed were the porch chairs. Sitting on the porch for the last time with friends I loved, was bittersweet. Tears, laughter, and sweet reminiscing closed the chapter of fifteen years in Maryland. We had shared victories, defeats, and grown in God's grace. Personal times of great weariness were often put aside when the love for each other would stir us to encourage them a rainbow would come.

II Timothy 4:2 teaches us to be instant (prepared) in season and out of season (KJV). God has no downtime and uses His children to be the cause and effect of His light as we encourage others along life's way.

*****

~ From Nancy:

It was raining the day Glen and I met. He was carrying a box of books and struggling to open the door to our retail establishment. He spoke as if his words had been carefully chosen for the awkward entrance while dripping water was puddling on the floor.

Later in the day, after Glen had his books and table organized, I observed he became comfortable and at ease. When time allowed, I made my way to the table to investigate just what was creating the animated conversations between customers and Glen. It was obvious he had a passion for sharing his knowledge and pulling a desire to know more about history, life, and the Lord from those so inclined to chat. Each visit to Gettysburg and each book signing was consistent with the lug and tug first day we met.

He always carried his boxes of books and strived with care to encourage those who had a literary interest to grow more, and share more. Always, he readily encouraged strangers and friends, to recognize that their life had worth. There is a story waiting to be penned in every life, from Glen's point of view.

Throughout the years we have shared many highs and lows about our lives. His concern for others is genuine. He would always ask, "Why is that?" when something was amiss in your life. He knows there is always an answer, standing ready to be touched. It is his nature to act as the prod to make you think deeper, meditate, and pray.

His countenance changes when his submission to the Lord's anointing and inspired talent touches the piano keyboard. If you only know him as an author, your life is lacking. When the music that can refresh your soul and delight your heart resonates across the room, you only hope it will not cease.

~ Nancy Sidock, December, 2021

~ From Glen:

On one of my trips to Gettysburg, Pennsylvania, I enjoyed the pleasure of meeting Nancy Sidock and members of her family. They owned and operated a restaurant on the "Diamond" in downtown, old Gettysburg. This was a unique and historical place. I loved going there several times, visiting, purchasing, and signing Glen Aubrey authored Lincoln books for customers. Many customers came. We valued this experience.

What delicious meals I enjoyed from Nancy's kitchen! Really exceptional. I also was highly privileged to meet and greet James Getty in person, in their bookstore. Mr. Getty *was* "Lincoln" to thousands, representing Steven B. Wiley and The Lincoln Leadership Institute at Gettysburg. Jim Getty was an icon. What an honor to make his acquaintance.

Nancy and I shared much; I purchased many volumes for my Lincoln library from that store. They remain in the library as unique treasures.

Nancy was (and is) a thoughtful, effective "prayer warrior," praying for some in my presence with a sincerity and passion I admired, and she was a wise giver of health, literally, with medicines of her own making, and an encourager.

It was an honor to receive and include her chapter for *God's Promises * Every One Fulfilled*. You can feel the poetry of her soul shining through.

~ Glen Aubrey, October, 2021

*****

God Never Gave Up on Me

Skip Vaccarello
Author: *Finding God in Silicon Valley * Spiritual Journeys*
In A High-Tech World
https://skipvaccarello.com/
Published by Creative Team Publishing, 2015
www.creativeteampublishing.com

As I reflect on my 73 years of life, I have a profound sense of thanksgiving. I am most appreciative for God's grace. He never gave up on me, although I set Him aside for twenty years and lived a life centered on the pursuit of success and achievement.

I also have a sense of how short life is, and how precious relationships are. I heard a quote once that still resonates with me. It went something like this, "All that matters in the end — that is, when we die — is how much we loved other people, how much we were loved, and what we did about God."

I am eternally grateful for having found God--who was always there, but of whom I took little notice — and for the mission God gave to me: to help other people know who He is.

And I am deeply thankful for the blessing of family and friends along with the opportunities granted to me, to use my gifts, talents, and resources to affect others positively.

Like everyone, I have suffered disappointments and failures. But, for the most part, I have learned from them. God opened new opportunities for me, including my unlikely career in Silicon Valley.

Here Is My Story

There is a sense that anything can happen in Silicon Valley. With hard work, one great idea can become a million-dollar company. Silicon Valley is the place where dreams come true, companies come to life, and today's failure may lead to tomorrow's great success. The sky is the limit. Many an innovator has seen their cutting-edge idea bring notoriety as well as fortune. Adventure, success, and wealth are synonymous with Silicon Valley.

My wife, Jackie, and I were excited about the possibilities Silicon Valley offered when we moved there from the East Coast in 1979. But, in doing so, we had to leave behind friends and family and an area we both loved. I had lived my whole life in New England and Jackie had lived much of her life there, too.

My Upbringing

I was born in 1948 and grew up in Waltham, Massachusetts, a city of 55,000 people ten miles west of Boston. It was made up primarily of second- and third-generation immigrant families — predominately Italian, Irish, and French Canadian. For a city of its size, Waltham was a surprisingly close-knit town. Many had relatives living there. In addition, local politics and the love of local sports teams from Little League through high school were two threads that knit the city even closer together.

My parents moved to Waltham shortly after they were married, to live in a two-bedroom apartment owned by my dad's aunt. That is where I was born. We moved to a larger home when my mom was pregnant with my brother. Although large to us, it was a small home by today's standards — three bedrooms and one bath. My brother and I slept in the same bed, while my sisters shared another bedroom. It was a comfortable home on a tree-lined, dead-end street that backed up to a playground. The playground had two baseball diamonds, a basketball court, fields for football, and a play area with seesaws and swings for children. I spent nearly every waking hour on that playground. My childhood revolved around sports — baseball in the spring and summer, football in the fall, and basketball in the winter.

I thrived on competition and even made-up games when the weather was bad. I played football in the snow and basketball in my basement. I made a hoop out of the ring of a coffee container, coated it with tin foil so we wouldn't cut our hands, nailed it to a rafter, and used a softball to play. When alone, I played baseball on my bed. I used baseball cards for the players, a pencil and marble for the bat and ball, and shoeboxes and books for the fences. The Red Sox won nearly every one of those games.

I was blessed with parents who loved and cared for me. They showed their love in many ways—coming to nearly all my games, taking an interest in what I was doing, and sacrificing to pay for family vacations.

My mom was Protestant; my dad was Catholic. Since my mom and dad were married by a Catholic priest in a Catholic church, my mom agreed to raise her children in the Catholic Church. My neighborhood was predominately Catholic—Irish and Italian—with a few Jewish kids mixed in. The playground was abandoned on Wednesday afternoons as the Catholic kids were in "Sunday School" at our local church. My most distinct memories of those classes were how afraid I was of the nuns and how I struggled to memorize the Baltimore Catechism. However, I can still recite the beginning of the Catechism. "Who made us? God made us. Who is God? He is the Supreme Being, who made all things …" I had a real sense of God as a child, but He seemed to fade away into my childhood memories after high school.

In my senior year at Waltham High School, I was co-captain of the football team, which went undefeated and tied for the Class A championship in eastern Massachusetts. In addition, I was the co-winner of the Most Valuable Player award and won the league scoring title. Although I was small at 5′ 9″and 160 pounds, some colleges recruited me to play football. The University of Connecticut (UConn) offered me a full four-year scholarship. I was intrigued, however, by a vice president at Yale who suggested that if I took a year at Phillips Exeter Academy in New Hampshire and did well, I might be admitted to Yale. My parents, who earned only a modest income, encouraged me to apply to Exeter. They wanted the best for me, even if it meant more sacrifice for them. If admitted, I would, of course, be giving up a four-year scholarship to UConn.

I applied and was accepted to Exeter. It was a tough year. The academics were rigorous, but I performed well enough to interest top colleges, including Harvard, where I chose to attend. My path was set. Looking back, I can see how God had His hand on me even then, although I thought I was getting in on my own merits.

All of the students at Exeter were required to attend a religious service of their choice on weekends. I chose the Catholic service since I grew up Catholic. Students were required to sign in to make sure we were credited with attending. If we did not attend, we could be put under restrictions of some sort. The most popular religious service was "Jew Cong" — Jewish congregation — that met on Friday nights. Although there were not many Jewish students on campus, this was by far the most popular service. My classmates preferred sleeping in on Sunday mornings and getting their religious attendance requirement out of the way on Friday nights since there were no girls to date at this all-boys school anyway.

The Catholic upbringing of my early years was giving way to feeling disconnected from faith and church. The services offered little meaning to me. Religion seemed to be about rules, which I often broke. I would go to confession, and within hours, I had sinned again. Rather than feeling consumed with guilt, I disengaged. Later in life, I realized that faith is not about adherence to rules — which are often man-made and not biblical — but about a relationship with Christ.

> Later in life, I realized that faith is not about adherence to rules — which are often man-made and not biblical — but about a relationship with Christ.

The required worship attendance added to my growing disenchantment with organized religion. This was the beginning of a twenty-year hiatus from the practice of faith.

When I entered Harvard in the fall of 1967, God was the last thing on my mind. My four years at Harvard were turbulent years on campus and in the country. Like many other college students at the time, Harvard students were ardently against the War in Vietnam. The draft made the issue personal for many, including me. During my time at Harvard, there was a riot in Harvard Square, university buildings were taken over, a student strike shut down classes, and business recruiters—especially those associated with the war effort— were blocked from coming on campus. The staid halls of Harvard were caught up in the protests as students wanted to bring attention to the university's support for the war effort and its perceived anti-women and racist policies. It was a season of change and discontent. Nathan Pusey, the Harvard President at the time, was quoted as calling my class—the class of 1971— "the worst class ever."

The turmoil of the early 70s deeply affected my classmates and me. In contrast to earlier Harvard classes in which around 90% of the graduates went on to graduate schools, only 62% of my classmates went on to graduate school immediately after graduation. Many of us "dropped out" and took non-traditional jobs for Harvard graduates—cab driver, farmer, bartender, and fisherman. Some did not work at all. It took us a while to find our bearings, but within five years, a study showed that, like previous Harvard graduates, 90% of our class had attended or were attending graduate schools. It simply took time for my classmates and me to get our lives together after all the turbulence we experienced at college.

An Unusual Path to Silicon Valley

I graduated with a concentration in economics. Although I was attracted to business activities, I could not see myself working for a large company. Instead, starting and running a small business interested me. After graduation, a couple of classmates and I started a waterbed business — my first start-up, if you can call it that. We were not particularly committed to the company, and it was not successful. We earned less than $2,000 and folded it within a couple of months.

After abandoning the waterbed business in the fall of 1971 and working at some part-time jobs to make money, I took a position at a nonprofit organization with a mission to help mentally disabled adults and their families. I continued in that field with three different nonprofits over seven years, culminating in a two-year stint as the Executive Director of the newly formed nonprofit named the Arthur J. Clark Workshop in Waltham. That was my second start-up.

In 1973, I began attending the Boston University School of Management part-time while working full time. I earned my MBA in 1977. It was a grind to work full time and attend graduate school part-time. However, the best part of business school was meeting my future wife, Jackie. She was an attractive, intelligent Wellesley graduate. Although we were both dating other people, we became friends over beer at the local bars after class. We hit it off immediately. We found it easy to talk with each other and shared similar values, especially about the importance of family and friends. Neither of us took ourselves too seriously. Although we sometimes had discussions on serious topics, we shared a sense of humor. We started dating exclusively in 1975 and married in 1978.

All the pieces of my life were falling into place. I had finished business school, was making a reasonable living, and married a wonderful woman. Then, opportunity came knocking. Just a year after getting married, the founders of a start-up company in personal computing software called Personal Software asked me to join them as they prepared to move the company from the Boston area to Silicon Valley. Even though my only exposure to software was an introductory programming course I took as an MBA student, I was fascinated by these new machines—the Commodore Pet, Radio Shack's TRS-80, and of course, the Apple II. The games were fun to play—especially Microchess, which was developed by Peter Jennings, one of Personal Software's founders. However, what interested me more than the games was a product in development—an electronic spreadsheet, later named VisiCalc. Up to that point, the personal computer industry was small and dominated by engineering types. I could see that this electronic spreadsheet would open the world of personal computing to the masses. It provided a simple way to put together financial forecasts, personal budgets, and even bowling averages. I wanted in.

Dan Fylstra, an MIT and Harvard Business School graduate, was Personal Software's other founder. He spearheaded the effort to develop the spreadsheet with the spreadsheet's originators and developers, Dan Bricklin and Bob Frankston of Software Arts. I am not sure what Peter and Dan saw in me. Perhaps it was my interest and enthusiasm for their business and potential for VisiCalc. Maybe they saw my leadership capabilities in running the nonprofit. Certainly, it was not my technical capabilities. Nevertheless, they asked me to join them as their first full-time employee. I was excited to do so and to embark on a new career in an innovative industry.

Jackie was also ready for a new adventure. She had been working in a Boston bank and was not that enthusiastic about her boss. Because one of my sisters was living in San Jose, the thought of making the transition to California was easier for us. We would have family close by, we would have each other, and we would have a new start in an amazing new community.

In the spring of 1979, I started as the Vice President of Operations at Personal Software — later renamed VisiCorp. This was my third start-up. It was an exciting time to work in the industry in its infancy. But Silicon Valley was different from Boston — not just the weather and landscape, but the culture.

Coming from Boston with its fanaticism about politics and sports, I was surprised by the lack of interest in either—especially politics. Instead, cocktail talk was about high-tech companies poised to take advantage of the most recent innovations. The heroes were high-tech company executives, not the candidates for office. Yes, you could hear such discussion, but compared to what I had experienced in Boston, the contrast was dramatic. Whereas in Boston, politics dominated the news, the Bay Area news focused on local crime with barely a mention of politics. The San Jose Mercury News had an entire business section dedicated to high-tech information. Boston radio had multiple sports talk stations. The Bay Area had one.

In Silicon Valley at the time, people were quick to move from one company to another to take a job at a company with the next greatest technology or with a path to going public. Unlike New England, the college you attended was less important than what you could do. The casual dress belied the intense work environment. People worked very hard and for long hours.

As with most start-ups, my job included doing a range of activities. I loved the challenge and the excitement to be part of something new. VisiCalc was introduced to the market in the fall of 1979 on the Apple II, and became a hit almost overnight. Steve Wozniak, Apple's co-founder, attributed VisiCalc as one of the two factors—the other was the floppy disk—which accounted for the Apple II success.

As the company grew, so did my responsibilities. Work consumed most of my time. I had to adapt from my 9-5 routine at the nonprofit to working 12 hours per day in this Silicon Valley start-up. Jackie took a position as a financial analyst at another Silicon Valley company. But there was a different, new adventure beckoning us: parenthood. In 1982, Jackie left the workforce and became a full-time mom when our first daughter, Julia, was born.

The next three years, from 1982 through 1985, were a period of transition. I took over as president of Communications Solutions, Inc. (CSI), a newly acquired subsidiary of VisiCorp, where I joined the CSI founders in running this networking and communications company. In 1985, our second daughter, Christina, was born.

When we moved to Silicon Valley, Jackie and I had a meager net worth, most of which was in our home's equity. However, by the mid-1980s, our net worth had dramatically increased. We had two beautiful daughters and owned a four-bedroom house in Los Altos, an upscale town located in the heart of Silicon Valley. Life was good. I had everything a man could ever want. But somehow, I did not feel fulfilled. Something was missing.

I had everything a man could ever want. But somehow, I did not feel fulfilled. Something was missing.

"A God-Shaped Vacuum"

Even though I longed for success and appreciated the money I earned, I sensed that there was more to life than business, competition, and success. I didn't know what. What more could I possibly want in life—perhaps more money? The miracle of birth—especially the birth of our first child—caused me to pause and think about God and life. "Who is this God? What role does He have in my life?" These were the questions I asked. But the busyness of life—long hours at work and now helping to raise our children—caused those thoughts to fade into the background.

Occasionally, in the quiet moments of life—just before going off to sleep or looking at a mountain range or a sunset—I would ponder who God was and what life was about. While success and money were good, I was finding they offered no long-term satisfaction.

There was a void in my life that I couldn't fill on my own. Centuries earlier, mathematician and philosopher Blaise Pascal identified the feeling I was experiencing as "a God-shaped vacuum" that is in each of us. I knew there had to be more to life. I needed God but didn't know it. Success was good, but not all I thought it would be. What was I missing?

These thoughts were leading me down a path toward God. I had rejected the rules that dominated my childhood faith, but had discovered no new faith. I was unsure of what

I believed. Here I was, a successful man in most people's eyes, but I found it wasn't enough. I needed to know if there was more. I asked, "Is God real? Is there evidence to prove that He exists?" I had come full circle. Did those catechism questions of my youth have the answers: "Who made us? Who is God? ..."

Little did I know that this was my new journey--a journey of finding out that God is real, that He loved me, had opened doors of opportunity for me, and had a purpose for my life.

> ... this was my new journey--a journey of finding out that God is real, that He loved me, had opened doors of opportunity for me, and had a purpose for my life.

Although I sometimes thought about God, I did nothing to seek Him out, that is, until 1985 after the birth of Christina. In July, she was born with a genetic condition that required close monitoring, necessitating blood tests every other day and then weekly. The stress for Jackie to bring Christina and three-year-old Julia to the hospital to watch the nurses prick Christina's heel to draw a small tube of blood left Jackie and the kids in tears.

The invitation to Julia by a friend to attend Vacation Bible School (VBS), as well as the offer to pick her up and take her home for the two-week program, was an immense relief to Jackie. Finally, she could focus on Christina's needs. I was comfortable with Julia attending VBS, since I'd had a positive experience in a VBS session as a child.

The timing of the invitation to VBS and its impact on our lives by bringing us into a church family was an amazing example of God's grace that we didn't recognize at the time. Julia loved VBS and asked when she could return to the church. However, we did nothing about church until later that summer when a neighbor invited Jackie to attend a church service — on a weekend when I was on a business trip in Paris.

When I called home to see how Jackie and the children were doing, much to my surprise, Jackie told me she had attended church. "You did what?" I asked. She repeated that she had gone to church. I was astounded. She explained how much she enjoyed the peace she felt at church and how much Julia enjoyed Sunday School.

Soon Jackie began attending church on a fairly regular basis. At one point, I agreed to "try" church with her. Some of my reluctance in attending was because this was a Protestant church. Having grown up as a Catholic, I was not sure what to expect at this church. I was also aware of what I had been taught — that the Roman Catholic Church was the only true church. But the years of not attending any church softened my resistance. I felt surprisingly comfortable in this church. Although I do not remember the sermon's content that Sunday, I do recall that Pastor Kent Mead's message aroused my curiosity about faith. And the people were friendly. They were not weird and, in fact, looked like other Silicon Valley people. I also noticed that the church had several families with young children.

A Decision for Christ

I began to attend with Jackie. As I did, Kent Meads' messages began resonating with me. He applied biblical principles to real-life situations to which I could relate. As a result, I began to read the Bible seriously. Up to that point, my only real exposures to the Bible were passages I had heard at the Catholic church I attended as a child, and in a "Bible as Literature" course I had taken at Harvard. I also began researching the evidence for the Christian faith by reading various books, including some by Josh McDowell and C.S. Lewis. I took an adult Sunday School class on the Bible and asked many questions. The Old Testament prophesies that were fulfilled by Jesus and the evidence for the resurrection were particularly convincing to me.

Over the next several months, I overcame most of my doubts—although I still had many questions—and accepted Christ as my Savior. I did not answer an altar call or anything like that. I simply accepted the truth of the Bible and vowed to learn more. The year was 1986. Jackie made a similar decision at roughly the same time. My decision was at first intellectual—it made sense by what I read and noticed in the world around me.

When I have told this story, I would feel somewhat embarrassed. I did not have any immediate vision or emotional acceptance of Christ. But I realized years later that other people, including C.S. Lewis, the renowned Christian intellectual and writer, had a similar experience of coming to faith, first based on the evidence.

> ... coming to faith, first based on the evidence.

Over the next few years, my faith deepened, and became emotional as well as intellectual. I began to understand the suggestion in I Thessalonians 5, to pray continually. Consequently, much of my thought life during the day was about God. My life's focus became how I could serve Christ—at home, in the workplace, through the church, and in the community—and at the same time, I developed a strong desire to help others know the joy that comes from having a personal relationship with Christ.

My career continued to advance following my conversion. We sold CSI three times to three different companies, the last time to 3Com in 1988, all at higher valuations. I stayed at 3Com for a year as a general manager before co-founding The Saratoga Group, a multimedia training company, with the two founders of CSI. This was my fourth start-up. In 2000, we sold that company to Channelwave Software, where I stayed for a year. I worked from 2001 into 2008 as a consultant and executive coach before taking the position as president and

CEO of Applied Weather Technology (AWT), a company providing software and services for the maritime industry. I worked at AWT from 2008 through 2012.

Success--or, rather, the lack of lasting fulfillment that comes from success — led to faith in Christ for me. What was missing for me was God. Once I came to faith, I realized that a fulfilling life is not about a string of achievements, power, or wealth. Faith and a relationship with Christ gave me an eternal perspective that helped provide context for whatever success or failure I experienced. Contentment was the result.

> Once I came to faith, I realized that a fulfilling life is not about a string of achievements, power, or wealth.
> Faith and a relationship with Christ gave me an eternal perspective that helped provide context for whatever success or failure I experienced.
> Contentment was the result.

This was not contentment with the way things are in this challenging world; rather, contentment knowing and believing **_His promise_** that I am a child of Christ, as expressed in John 1:12 — "But to all who believed him and accepted him, he gave the right to become children of God." (NLT)

~ *Holy Bible*, New Living Translation, copyright © 1996, 2004, 2015 by Tyndale House Foundation. Used by permission of Tyndale House Publishers, Inc., Carol Stream, Illinois 60188. All rights reserved.

This was also contentment knowing **_His promise_** for salvation— "For God so loved the world that he gave his one and only Son, that whoever believes in him shall not perish but have eternal life." (John 3:16)

Knowing God's Promises gave me a purpose to honor Him in all that I do. God gifted me with a mission to help others on their spiritual journeys.

My personal mission statement, which I first wrote in 2001, is this:

*To be a blessing and to serve other people.
I hope to encourage, inspire, and lead people
to faith in Jesus Christ,
and hope to use the platforms God gives me
to accomplish my mission.*

*****

Success takes on a new meaning. It is not about business, financial, or athletic achievements. Instead, success is about growing closer to Jesus and honoring Him in all that I do. Success is about living out God's calling for me as a husband, father, grandfather, friend, businessman, and member of my church and community. And success means following His call to help others on their spiritual journeys.

My mission leads me, among other things:

1. To engage in one-on-one discussions with not-yet-believers who are interested in exploring questions about faith
2. To have written *Finding God in Silicon Valley*
3. To chair the Silicon Valley Prayer Breakfast, now called Connect Silicon Valley (CSV).

> In short, the purpose of both my book and CSV is to encourage people to explore Christian faith.

CSV's vision is to see Silicon Valley become known not only as the center of innovation, entrepreneurship, technology, and wealth creation, but a place of God. We believe that if our vision were to become a reality, the world would take notice.

Our mission at CSV is to open up conversations about faith between those who believe and those who are skeptical. Our method is to host events, including our Annual Breakfast, which now attracts around 1,000 people. The events feature high-profile speakers, most of whom come from Silicon Valley. The speakers focus on their spiritual journeys and how Jesus is at the center of their lives and informs all they do.

Speakers have included:

1. Pat Gelsinger, now CEO of Intel
2. Condoleezza Rice, former United States Secretary of State (2005-2009)
3. Kirk Perry, formerly president of a Google division
4. Top venture capitalist Promod Haque

In addition to chairing Connect Silicon Valley, I am a partner in 1Flourish Capital, a venture firm focused on start-up companies. At 1Flourish, we believe that business is one meaningful way to impact the culture at large positively. Our mission is to invest in entrepreneurs of character who want to run their business the right way; that is, by following and applying biblical principles.

Studies have shown that businesses that are run the right way have a greater chance of success than those with a negative culture, burdened by distrust. At 1Flourish, we hope to bring a healthy financial return to our investors and a positive experience to all the constituents our portfolio companies touch, and to bring glory to God.

I also serve on boards, including Carpenter's Code, a for-profit company headquartered in Silicon Valley, with the most popular Christian meditation app called *Abide*. And I am a founding partner and elder at New Beginnings Community Church (NBCC), with campuses in Redwood City and San Jose. NBCC is an ethnically and culturally diverse Bible-believing church focusing on serving the community and reaching those who are not yet followers of Christ.

The guiding principles in my life since becoming a Christ-follower are Colossians 3:23 (NLT), which reads, "Work willingly at whatever you do, as though you were working for the Lord rather than for people," and I Peter 3:15, "Always be prepared to give an answer to everyone who asks you to give the reason for the hope that you have. But do this with gentleness and respect ..."

I try my best to represent Christ positively in the workplace, at home, and in the community. I know I fail sometimes, but I try my best to love everyone, whether or not they follow Christ. I have found that treating people with "gentleness and respect" is essential, and a prerequisite to encouraging them to consider faith in Jesus.

God fulfills His promises to touch others through Skip's life and testimony.
He will do this for anyone who commits his or her life to His leadership and His will, unreservedly.

*****

212

From Skip:

I had been exploring various ways of having my book published and was close to committing to a literary agent who represented some renowned Christian authors. But she wanted to take control of the project, having someone from outside Silicon Valley re-write the stories, and at my cost. I decided not to go with that option.

Shortly after I made the decision, I attended a men's conference sponsored by the New Canaan Society (NCS). At the conference, I met Retired Major General Bob Dees at a breakout session he led. Bob had several books he wrote on display. I asked who he used for a publisher, and he replied, "Glen Aubrey of Creative Team Publishing." I contacted Glen and, after some discussion, agreed to have CTP publish my book, ***Finding God in Silicon Valley.***

~ Skip Vaccarello, July, 2021

From Glen:

Skip's book, ***Finding God in Silicon Valley * Spiritual Journeys In A High-Tech World*** is a book Creative Team Publishing was honored to publish. It is packed with life altering stories of spiritual commitments, where lives were changed, sometimes radically, for Christ. Regardless of a person's business and personal life, the differences Christ made in each convert was lasting and true. I strongly encourage you to obtain this book, and read it.

The life testimonies you'll view may help you make the same kind of redemptive faith commitment. This faith commitment will impact your world, as well as redeem you. *God's Promises* are fulfilled in Skip's life by giving him a purpose to honor God in all he does. God wants to do the same for you.

~ Glen Aubrey, July, 2021

*****

Challenges of God's Faithfulness

Larry Wolf
Retired L.A. County Sheriff
Criminal Justice Professor, University of Antelope Valley,
Lancaster, California
Author: *A Black and White Decision * Why George*
*Zimmerman Was Found Innocent * Why America Must*
Honor the Memory of Trayvon Martin
Policing Peace: What America Can Do Now to Avoid Future
Tragedies
*Word on the Street **
The Unexpected Realities of Police Work
www.policingpeace.com
Published by Creative Team Publishing, 2013, 2017,
respectively, with the
third book to be published in 2022.
www.creativeteampublishing.com

What would you do if one of the richest men in the world offered you a dream job with a salary of several million dollars a year? Would you not enthusiastically begin working for him and attempt to cash the first check?

What would you do if the all-powerful Creator of the universe offered you peace, purpose, and immortality?

And, that He made this offer with other promises that could be valuated and tested? Only a fool would not take a serious look into these promises.

Challenging God, and demanding proof from a sinful, unbelieving state are obviously not promising spiritual endeavors. However, the promises in God's Word, on many levels, are invitations from Almighty God to put Him to the test.

Is not Jesus' call to us in Revelation 3:20 exactly that? "Behold I stand at the door and knock: if anyone hears My voice and opens the door, I will come into him and dine with him, and he with Me." (NASB). Is this not a promise of God calling upon each of us to respond and experience a new life with His faithfulness and blessings?

The Bible encourages childlike faith. To those who repent and accept God's free gift of salvation, living by faith in every moment becomes the backdrop from which God's faithfulness can be experienced. But will He allow His faithfulness to be tested? I believe He will.

God's Call and His Promises

I became a believer in the Lord Jesus Christ in August of 1975. My conversion was profound and existential. It was the culmination of a two-year period during which

I became engaged in a "try it, you'll like it" proposition from believers who encouraged me to turn to the Lord.

Two sweet but naive Christian girls whom I constantly made fun of, were praying for me and my family. I playfully mocked them and their simple faith, only to find the joke was on me. After two years of highly-coincidental occurrences of positivity for me and my family, I was convinced beyond a reasonable doubt that these girls were right and I was wrong. More importantly, I was convinced there was a God, that He loved me, and that He was helping me.

Great Faithfulness

I was soon introduced to authentic Christian fellowship, old style worship, and classic Christian hymns. Some of the songs were simple and some were bordering on hokey. But I came to love them. I sang the songs heartily as part of my penance, having experienced a cosmic "I told you so" for doubting.

I also dutifully tried to put into practice popular Christian catch phrases like "Give it to God" and the tried-and-true gem "Let go and let God." I playfully mocked myself as I sang, prayed, and tried to put into practice the simplest of Christian concepts. Was I naïve and deluded?

My life was changed forever and since then I have experienced more than forty years of God's faithfulness. The classic hymn "Great Is Thy Faithfulness" serves as an anthem of God's promises and all that he has done for me.

Three Challenges

The following exercises in Christian living soon became part of my life, and in some ways represent tests of God's promises and faithfulness.

1) **"Give it to God"—Trusting God to help in every situation**

The Bible proclaims God's faithfulness. Of the countless promises contained in His Word perhaps none is more important than His promise to save those who call upon His name. "Everyone who calls on the name of the Lord will be saved" is referenced in both Romans 10:13 and Acts 2:21 (NASB).

The general context of this promise appears to be for a person's initial salvation. Additionally, the expectation of God's faithfulness when believers call upon His name in other matters seems well supported scripturally.

The challenge, simply put, is to sincerely pray and seek God's help in any situation. Expect and evaluate what happens when you truly give something to God; not as a sinful, unbelieving challenge; rather, as a sincere call upon the Lord with the opportunity, and in anticipation, of experiencing His faithfulness.

And yes, we must be careful when we evaluate all the little miracles or coincidences that we might come to believe in when we are walking closely with God. Still, I believe most Christians will see a distinct pattern in the quality and happiness of their lives when they trust and live by faith vs. when they stray and walk in darkness. This difference is part of God's covenant promises and also demonstrates His faithfulness.

2) "I'll pray for you"

Another test of God's faithfulness is trusting Him to work His will and way when we pray for others. I used to be afraid to let people know I was praying for them. On some levels, I didn't trust what the Lord might allow to happen. I guess I was afraid things might get worse. I didn't want me or the Lord left holding the spiritual bag.

Over the years, more and more, I came out of the closet and told people I was praying for them even in the face of tragedy and hardship. Truly this is putting God's promises and faithfulness to the test.

To my surprise, invariably people, even non-believers, would sincerely thank me when I told them I was praying for them. Most would indulge me and let me say a prayer for them out loud while they listened or better yet would indicate they were in agreement with the prayer.

Often, we as Christians try to win the debate explaining how someone can be saved. The "Roman Road" or a solid Bible tract might indeed be the vehicle God uses to bring someone to Himself. But praying for someone confidently in faith might also be the beginning point for someone being led into the kingdom.

We should put God's promises and faithfulness to the test even when we pray for others.

3) Giving/Tithing

One of the disciplines of a Godly life, is giving. Tithing — the giving of ten percent of one's earnings to God or the church, is encouraged by most evangelical congregations. Putting this into practice provides another area that can demonstrate God's faithfulness.

God has promised to care for all of our needs. Giving back some of the material blessings we have received seems only natural. Yet giving during financial hardship seems counter to logic and provides the Christian with a unique test of faith.

Giving during times of financial hardship is a particularly difficult spiritual discipline. But when done as part of a faith-based life, it's yet another test of God's faithfulness.

I have heard about of countless examples of people who gave when it wasn't easy and seemed to be rewarded for their faithfulness. An unexpected check miraculously came in the mail after someone tithed when it hurt or a job offer materialized, etc.

Some of the anecdotal evidence might seem childlike and contrived. At the same time, who among us has experienced the opposite, that living a Godly life and giving has resulted in financial ruin or caused personal disaster? I can think of none.

Put God's promises and faithfulness to the test by giving.

A Final Thought

I was literally embarrassed when I considered the juvenile simplicity of what I had written, compared to some of the more profound concepts found elsewhere in this book.

Having childlike faith is humbling intellectually. Yet some of mankind's greatest minds have found peace, purpose, and true knowledge of God at the foot of the cross within a relationship to the Lord Jesus Christ. It is only there we will be able to experience first-hand the faithfulness of God and His promises.

*****

From Larry:

I met Glen Aubrey nearly forty years ago while managing a fitness center in San Diego, California. I was an aspiring song writer and much to my delight, I found out that Glen was an accomplished composer and arranger. I had some material that really needed work. Glen took my better songs and made them really good, and helped make my weaker compositions tolerable!

Eventually we produced an album and several other musical projects, including **End of Watch,** a song for downed peace officers used to memorialize officers killed on 9/11. During our collaboration on musical and literary projects over the years, Glen has become a mentor and dear friend.

I have been blessed to continue working with Glen on his latest project, "God's Promises." Having read most of the material included in this work, I have learned even more about the Lord, including most importantly — He *is* faithful. You can count on it.

~ Larry Wolf, November, 2021

From Glen:

Larry Wolf and I became acquainted in the 1980s. Our relationship began when I was working out in a local gym in San Diego, and Larry was my coach.

I sensed in this man a truly giving heart, and warmed to his spirit. If anything, I sought a relationship with Larry, believing we both would benefit in multiple ways, personally and professionally. Through the years we have experienced many music endeavors together: arranging, orchestrating, and producing his original songs, a dramatic musical album, including *End of Watch*, and now publishing three of his original books, following the conclusion of his career as a Los Angeles County Sheriff, and in recognition of his tenure as a Criminal Justice professor at the University of Antelope Valley, Lancaster, California:

1. *A Black and White Decision * Why George Zimmerman Was Found Innocent * Why America Must Honor the Memory of Trayvon Martin*
2. *Policing Peace: What America Can Do Now to Avoid Future Tragedies*
3. *Word on the Street * The Unexpected Realities of Police Work*

Our experiences together are vast, and for these, and our association on many levels, I am profoundly grateful.

~ Glen Aubrey, November, 2021

*****

223

Postlude

The Covenant:
God's Fulfillment
Is a Binding Contract with Us

II Chronicles 7:14

"... if my people, who are called by my name, will humble themselves and pray and seek my face and turn from their wicked ways, then I will hear from heaven, and I will forgive their sin and will heal their land."

When Creative Team Publishing was formed in 2007, we chose to *not* use contracts with any of our authors. See www.creativeteampublishing.com. We have been faithful to that commitment from day one. Our authors were told that we wanted to work with people who wanted to work with us, and that a contract would never be used to "guarantee" that either author or publisher would fulfill required duties, including fiscal responsibility. Rather, a "word is our bond" agreement was instituted. It was iron-clad then and is iron-clad now.

No author has ever been requested or expected to sign a contract. Ever.

With more than 80 titles in print, the formula has worked. It has worked because all of us, Publishers and Authors, chose to trust each other. The actions of both publisher and author demonstrate this fact.

Consider God's Promises to us, however. We *do* have a binding contract from God of which we are a part. We endeavor to honor that contract with our whole being.

That contract is voiced in Scripture and has proven reliable. God's fulfillment occurs daily in the promises He has made, and continues to make. The stories in this book, all of them true, are simply reminders of that foundation. While varied, they all illustrate in contemporary, real life, this everlasting truth: ***God's Promises * Every One Fulfilled***.

God instituted a binding contract, or covenant, with His children. This binding contract states that if and when His people fulfill their parts of the covenant, His promises are fulfilled.

Let's examine the II Chronicles scripture more fully.

It begins, quoting God, "… if my people …" Those of us who believe in God, belong to God. We are His. Further, we are called by His Name. The name of the triune God is stamped on our new birth certificate. Yes, we indelibly belong to Him, eternally.

This scripture comes to mind in Romans 8:38, 39 (KJV):

> [38] For I am persuaded, that neither death, nor life, nor angels, nor principalities, nor powers, nor things present, nor things to come, [39] Nor height, nor depth, nor any other creature, shall be able to separate us from the love of God, which is in Christ Jesus our Lord.

That's everlasting. No separation from God for His children is a *guarantee* for "His kids" from their Lord, their Creator.

In II Chronicles 7:14, responsibilities to uphold this contract begin for God's children after God's "ownership" of His people is declared. The actions are stated unequivocally:

1. God's people must humble themselves: I have been awe-struck, realizing that God does not do the humbling, though He often may create or allow circumstances to open the doors for us to choose humility. Humbling oneself is primary; there can be no wrongful pride or inappropriate self-aggrandizement which exceeds true human worth because all of us are made "in the image of God." (Genesis 1:27). Human dignity and personhood of individuals, as children of

God is a characteristic of the created ones, and it is best seen when God's people serve, not exalting themselves. Jesus, in Matthew 23:11, taught this: "The greatest among you will be your servant." Interestingly, Jesus goes on to say, in the next verse: "For those who exalt themselves will be humbled, and those who humble themselves will be exalted." Therefore, we humble ourselves before God and each other. The admonition to do so is found in the writings of James and Peter.

From the letter of James, James 4:10 (KJV)

> Humble yourselves in the sight of the Lord, and he shall lift you up.

And from I Peter 5:6 (KJV)

> Humble yourselves therefore under the mighty hand of God, that he may exalt you in due time:

What these verses declare: *we* do the personal humbling and ***God*** does the exalting!

2. Pray: prayer is talking with God. Prayer puts the one praying in the right position to God, in humility, as requesters, intercessors, praising God for His lordship and our willful dependence upon Him. The greatest

example of prayer was what Jesus taught when His disciples asked Him to teach them to pray.

Recorded in Matthew 6:9-13, the familiar verses are these:

> ⁹ "This, then, is how you should pray:
> "'Our Father in heaven, hallowed be your name,
> ¹⁰ your kingdom come, your will be done,
> on earth as it is in heaven.
> ¹¹ Give us today our daily bread.
> ¹² And forgive us our debts, as we also have forgiven our debtors.
> ¹³ And lead us not into temptation, but deliver us from evil; for yours is the kingdom and the power and the glory forever. Amen.'"

Prayer begins with a declaration of the Lordship of God, the Father; His holiness ("hallowed" literally means "consecrated" or "set apart"); we state our desire for His Kingdom to come, along with His will followed and obeyed, on the earth and in heaven. He alone is our daily provider; He alone forgives our sins, and models the forgiveness we share with others; He does not lead us into temptation; rather, delivers us from evil. Finally, we declare His Kingdom, power, and glory forevermore.

3. <u>Seek His face</u>: the phrase really means to earnestly desire His presence. This "seeking" includes <u>repentance</u> (agreeing with God on the person, work, and deity of Christ*), beginning with <u>confession</u>. Confession is ownership of wrongdoing. Confession includes humility. Confession is followed by a desire and request for forgiveness from "wicked ways." Repentance literally means "to turn from wrongdoing and go another way, the way of the Lord. We earnestly desire to see who Christ really is, and follow Him." Repenting from wicked ways is a reversal from thoughts and activities in direct contrast to the will of God; it's a turning *from* disobedience in all forms *to* His will, way, and plans. We alter our views about Christ. We follow Him.

   *This explanation of this word 'repentance' I learned from Pastor Robert Morris, Gateway Church, Southlake, Texas, in 2021. We change our attitudes and conclusions about who Christ is, and He changes our hearts.

When God's people return to Him in contrition as the prodigal son did, recorded in Luke 15:11-32, God promises to accomplish His plan for His people. Again, He has fulfilled every promise. Take comforts in these assurances.

He states:

1. "<u>I will hear from heaven</u> …" God literally pays the closest attention to His creation, whether or not His creation knows this, accepts, or believes this. He is not inattentive. We all know how inattentiveness feels, as receivers and givers. The opposite of inattentiveness is paying attention; listening deeply. What an honor and true blessing that God hears us without interruption! Is this not an example of how we should communicate with each other?

2. "<u>I will forgive their sin</u> …" God's forgiveness entails several results. Among them: Psalm 103:12: "… as far as the east if from the west, so far has he removed our transgressions from us." It's a long way between east and west--immeasurable. Transgressions are erased when God forgives. Memories may remain, but a perpetrator's account is wiped clean, permanently. This action also become the model of our treatment of others. Matthew 6:14, Jesus speaking: "For if you forgive other people when they sin against you, your heavenly Father will also forgive you." Forgiveness literally means "no longer holding an account open." It's a full and complete pardon.

3. "… <u>and heal their land</u>." This speaks of restoration of the former character of God's initial blessings: on anyone, his or her persons and possessions; it's

restitution; it is a return to health. This health is for "the land" and those people (His children) who occupy it and dwell within it. Broad interpretations are appropriate, I believe.

When we gaze intently into the character of God, we observe in perfect, flawless illustration how we should live and interact with each other, following the model of Jesus Christ. God's fulfillment and our obedience go hand in hand. In the same way Jesus was in submission to His Father, we submit to Jesus, fully assured of His love, promises, and fulfillments.

This binding contract never fails. It stands all tests of time … all time. It endures through all of life's victories or vicissitudes.

> God's fulfillment and our obedience go hand in hand.

*****

The Centrality of Christ

What is a culmination and final declaration of God's Promises? A capstone, cornerstone, reassuring, and affirming passage is recorded in II Corinthians 2, verse 20. It reads:

> [20] For no matter how many promises God has made, they are "Yes" in Christ. And so through

him the "Amen" is spoken by us to the glory of God.

God's promises are fulfilled in Christ. He is the center of every promise and every fulfillment, ultimately. Yes, He is the final conclusion of all.

> All of God's promises are fulfilled in Christ.

"Amen" literally means, "So be it." According to Merriam-Webster: amen is "solemn ratification (as an expression of faith) or hearty approval (as of an assertion)." Or, as one young lady who worked with me often said, "Done and done!" Complete, final, perfect, witnessed, approved. And it is in totality for the glory, edification, and praise of God.

Trusting wholeheartedly in God's Promises is not a far-fetched and "hope-inspired" concept or theory. It's a literal, down-to-earth, provable reality in a God who never wavers or fails.

Conclusion

God is eternal. God is also good. He is beyond comprehension. Yet, He desires a "closer than a brother" relationship with us!

Those who know Him, trust Him. God has never not honored His promises to His people. His promises and fulfillments align with the lasting characteristics of His existence.

Note Psalm 103:17, 18 (author emphasis):

> **17** But from <u>everlasting to everlasting</u> the LORD's love is with those who fear him, and his righteousness with their children's children —
> **18** with those who keep his covenant and remember to obey his precepts.

How far is "from everlasting to everlasting?" The Bible is replete with expressions concerning God's eternal existence and activity.

God's love is demonstrated in innumerable ways. One way is in His forgiveness. He tells us we must forgive as we have been forgiven, exercising the forgiveness He has shown us. "… as far as the east is from the west …" That is how far He has removed our transgressions from us. Isn't that great news?

Seek God. Yearn for His presence in your life. Experience His forgiveness. An eternal attribute, forgiveness is immeasurable, as is God's love.

Can you and I trust a personal God of this magnitude? How can we not? The conclusion of the matter is this: Yes, we can trust Him and we will.

Amen!

*****

CPSIA information can be obtained
at www.ICGtesting.com
Printed in the USA
JSHW051346200222
23100JS00001B/35